How to Wholesale

Your Handcrafted Soap

From Kitchen Space to Marketplace

Benjamin D. Aaron

Info@howtosellsoap.com

www.howtosellsoap.com

Printed in the United States of America

First Printing, 2015

Ordering Information:

Wholesale sales. Special discounts are available on quantity purchases. For details, contact the publisher at the email address above.

ISBN-10: 0692464158

ISBN-13: 978-0-692-46415-1

Dedication

This book is dedicated to all of the handcrafted soapmakers bold enough to chase their dreams. There is so much creativity and uniqueness in our industry, and it shines through every single one of us.

How to Wholesale Your Handcrafted Soap

Contents

.

Acknowledgments

Thank you, Mom and Dad, for loving me. You are my best friends. I am grateful for you.

Thank you, Amanda Gail. You have shown me what it means to live a life worth living. We are on a journey that I could never have imagined before you came into my life.

Thank you friends, for putting up with all of my dreadful soap and business conversations!

Thank you, fellow soapmakers. You have shown me that I can create a new and better version of myself.

Thank you, donors. The Lovin' Soap Project would never have taken wings if it weren't for you. Thank you for your trust and your open-handed nature.

Introduction

I've had a lot of fun writing this book. Many memories have come to mind as the words hit the page. Wholesaling soap has been quite the challenge for me, not to mention running a full storefront that operates 70 hours per week. It has been at times painful, and other times so free that it never, ever feels like a "real job."

What I really hope to convey in this book are concepts that you can get down on paper and then improve upon, based on your current situation and business, as everyone of us has such a matchless and truly unique way of running our handcrafted soap and bodycare businesses. I have found so much joy, support and happiness through this industry. This book was written because of the countless (and wonderful) soapmakers that I have had the privilege of knowing over the years, and all of the specific questions they've had about selling soap.

I fully admit that in our cottage industry, I would be seen as simply a commodity-driven, "plain bars" soapmaker. I continue to be so enthralled and impressed by all of the creativity that comes out of our soapmaking community in terms of beauty, art and unrivaled design from batch to batch, soapmaker to soapmaker. Because I am myself so impressed with these designs and have a heart to help, one of my major passions is to help soap artists of all kinds get paid for the beautiful functional art that they produce, as what we make not only provides an invaluable quality and service by means of hygiene, but also craft. Meaningful craft.

This book is full of ideas on how to sell your handmade soap to retail outlets. If at any point in your reading voyage you would like to discuss and confer, I encourage you to do so. We are all in this together. There is more than enough room in our industry for everyone to succeed.

Thank you so much, and keep doing great things.

Benjamin | 816.352.8206

Email | info@howtosellsoap.com

Chapter 1

Let's Talk About Goals

Goals are everything in business and life. If you do not have goals, your business will fail. If you and everyone in your business do not know what the goals are, everyone will be wasting their time. **You simply cannot hit a target that does not exist**. Goals empower you. Having clearly defined, well-written goals that you view every day automatically puts you in the top 3 percent of successful, thriving entrepreneurs.

Two out of three people in the United States suffer from low self-esteem. I strongly believe that anyone can raise their self-esteem through setting clear, attainable goals. Talents and abilities make some people successful. **Though talents and abilities** *are* **important, but knowing what we want is even more important.** When we know what we want (having clearly defined goals), we can direct our energy and make choices toward the attainment of our specific goals. Attaining goals brings the setting of new goals (and new goals…), thus producing an on-going cycle of positive growth and achievement.

I have decided to put a chapter on goals in this book, and if read linearly, the aim is to help you lay the groundwork for all of the tasks forthcoming, as you can then set proper goals after each chapter. This book is about wholesaling soap; but if you do not establish clear goals with deadlines, along with all of the underpinning tasks that go along with your goals, this book will not help you in the least. **Goals are everything in business and in life.**

The goal-setting tactics below are broad in nature and example, but they can be applied to any and all aspects of your soapmaking and soap selling endeavors. The idea of this chapter is for you to absorb the following information about goals and then begin reading the rest of this book with determination and purpose-driven objectives. Everything read below can be applied to this book's ensuing information. Whether you are new to goal setting or you need a tune-up, follow these techniques to setting goals for the best possible outcomes.

Five Rules of Effective Goal Phrasing

Goals should not be written as if they are a grocery list that you will get to eventually. They should be phrased and written in such a way that evokes power and positive motivation. Following are my five rules to effective goal phrasing, with examples from common life pursuits:

1) Be Specific.

Casual goals create casualties. Do not kill your goal by being vague. **Your brain is a goal-seeking mechanism. Use it!** Give your subconscious a deep and invested vision of what you want, and be as specific as possible. For each goal you comprise, write a brief scenario that includes your five senses and the emotions you will have when the goal has been completed.

2) Use the Present Tense.

Your list of goals must be written in the present tense, as if they are happening right this very moment. This gives an alert to the subconscious to get busy and pay attention to the people, circumstances and events that might advance the completion of the goal. "I want to…" or "I hope to…" or "Maybe someday…" are not goals. They are hopeful wishes at best. **A successful entrepreneur never allows, "I wish…" to ever cross the corners of their mouth; they instead say, "I am…"** They write down what they want and seek it out with fervor, for successful entrepreneurs are 100 percent responsible for the results they acquire in life. **Demand the present moment of yourself and of your goals**. Write in the present tense.

3) Keep it Positive!

Which one of these sounds better?

— I want to get out of debt.

— I am proudly financially free!

Of course the second statement sounds better. This makes you feel good and it holds power. Not only is the first statement not even a goal, it is negative. The word itself, debt, has a negative connotation, literally. Avoid these types of words and instead focus on how you are going to feel when you accomplish this goal and state it so.

4) Use "I."

Again, writing down a lineup of meaningful goals is not to be written like a grocery list. Using "I" as the very first word in each goal signals the subconscious to the power of what you are writing. "I am" is also effective. I even go as far starting each goal with **"I am so grateful now that..."** After this initial written action, follow it with an action verb:

— I am so grateful now that I earn...
— I am so grateful now that I weigh...
— I am so grateful now that I sell...
— I am so grateful now that I am living...

5) Give Each Goal a Deadline.

Your deadline doesn't have to be exact, but it should be your best guess. Your deadlines must be realistic based on your goals. Give yourself enough time to accomplish what you've set out to do. **Most importantly, if you do**

not reach your goal in the time you have allotted, simply bump back your deadline and keep going.

Examples of Phrasing Goals

Poorly Stated Goals:

—— I want to lose 20 lbs.
—— I want to sell a lot of soap.
—— I want better relationships.

Well-Phrased Goals:

—— I proudly weigh 165 lbs. on or before September 1.
—— I successfully sell 1,000 bars per month beginning June 1.
—— I make five genuine and uplifting phone calls to friends and family on Friday the 5th at 3 p.m.

Phrasing your goals in a positive and meaningful way encourages and motivates you in a way that otherwise would lay dormant inside you. One of the biggest hurdles I have witnessed from soapmakers who are struggling with sales and revenue is that they have never actually put a dollar amount down on paper. Simply writing down your monthly, weekly, etc. revenue goals and phrasing it according to the five rules is half the battle! **Write down your goals, soapmaker!**

Activating the Habit of Goal Setting

Following is a technique I have used for many years now with incredible results. I get goose bumps just thinking about all of the life circumstances, events and people that manifested into my life at the perfect time after being diligent daily with the activity below. **If you take nothing else away from this book, I implore you to try this technique, and do not skip a day.**

First go purchase a brand new notebook. In a quiet and reflective state of mind, write out five to ten goals that you would like to accomplish within the next 12 months. These can be personal, business, family and relationships, career, community-driven, etc. Do not limit your goals to what you think others expect from you. Come original. Make these yours, through and through. Phrase each goal according to the five rules previously explained.

Now Take It One Step Further.

Each morning as you rise, write down your five to ten goals, implementing all of the techniques above. Do the same before bed.

Do this day after day, twice a day until the notebook is complete. Keep the notebook on your bedside table, and if you travel often, make sure it goes with you.

But here is the caveat. Never look at your prior list. Stretch your subconscious into remembering these important life events you have written down. Never look at the list of goals you have previously written in the notebook. Start a fresh new page at each writing session. If your list changes here and there from time to time, good. It should. The people, circumstances and events in your life are constantly ebbing and flowing.

There aren't too many constants in the world, so it is okay if your list looks different from one day (or week) to the next. It is okay for your list to change every once in a while. Allow for this flexibility. But I am willing to bet that over the course of a week or two or three, the top one or two goals on your list never change. **These are your biggest and most important goals**. Among the top two or three most important goals, you will be astonished at how much you really start positively dwelling on all of the things on your daily lists. By practicing this technique every day, without fail, you are inundating your subconscious. **You are saturating your brain with what it is you want. And the goal-seeking mechanism that is your brain is constantly attempting to create scenarios that will bring what it is you want into reality.**

Consider as You Read this Book...

Setting goals in such a way is certainly not required for you to reach an ample level of success wholesaling soap. I offer these tactics early on in this book so that your mind can wrap itself around the concept of making serious and concrete plans after learning something new and helpful. **You can read this book twenty times and know it front to back, but if you do not *apply* any of the concepts into your business situation, you are wasting your time.**

Even writing out your short-term future goals every day in such a way will create momentum for ALL of the goals you wish to carry out in your life and business. The notebook technique has had a profound effect on my life, as I've had notebooks filled from beginning to end with the most seemingly outlandish goals in them, and they have all come to pass. And I can guarantee you that these outlandish things would not have occurred if I hadn't practiced this daily method. I believe the success I've had in obtaining a storefront, entering into large, nationwide partnerships with several different retail chains and even traveling the world through The Lovin' Soap Project can all be directly related to how much I write down every day, in the present tense, what I want to see happen in my personal life and my business. I strongly encourage you to apply these techniques as you move through this book.

Chapter Summary

— **If you do not have goals, your business will fail.**
— When writing down your goals, remember the five phrasing rules:
  1. Be specific.
  2. Use the present tense.
  3. Keep it positive!
  4. Use "I."

    5.   Give each goal a deadline.

— Go purchase a brand new notebook. In a quiet and reflective state of mind, write out five to ten goals that you would like to accomplish within the next 12 months.

Now take it one step further.

Each morning as you rise, write down your five to ten goals, implementing all of the techniques above. Do the same before bed, but never look at your prior lists until the notebook is completed.

Chapter 2

What is Wholesale?

Wholesaling is simple. You are merely trading goods for profit. In our case, we are trading soap and bodycare products for profit.

In a traditional distributorship, the model might look like this:

The role of the traditional distributor is to move the product from manufacturer to market. In the case of handmade soap and bodycare products, the model looks more like this:

In this model, the soapmaker *is* the manufacturer and most often works as the distributor as well, supplying retail stores their handmade products directly. That is not to say a soapmaker couldn't supply enough soap to warrant using a distributor, but (usually) the sale price to distributors is less than desirable and the demand might exceed production capabilities. Thus, the following model still dominates our handcrafted industry:

As the proprietor of a wholesale soap business, you will obviously be making soap to sell at a profit; the only difference is that you'll be working in the business-to-business realm by selling to retail companies and not to the buying public. The field of wholesale distribution requires good negotiation skills, a nose for sniffing out the next "hot" item in the soap and bodycare industry and keen sales-man/womanship. **The idea is to make soap at the lowest possible price and create your profit by tacking on a dollar amount that still makes the deal attractive to your customer, as they will need to tack on a dollar amount suitable for their store.**

A quick note about consignment…

Consignment is not wholesale. Under a wholesale agreement, you are selling your soap and bodycare products to a store and getting paid for it. If you consign your soap and bodycare products with a store, you are giving your items to the store and will only be paid once an item is sold to an end consumer. Though there are advantages to both, if you really want to move your business forward in a professional manner, wholesaling is by far the most advisable, and will be the subject matter of this book.

The cornerstone of the soap distribution cycle is the flow of product from the manufacturer (your company) to the end customer. As a wholesaler, your position on this supply chain is three-fold; 1) you handcraft quality soap and bodycare products at a reasonable price and then 2) sell them to the companies that need them. 3) Then you follow-up and allow for feedback to build a well-founded relationship with your new retail buyer.

Wholesaling soap is a long-term investment. Often you have to hustle, make phone calls, emails, make more phone calls, fill out paperwork and make more phone calls to acquire a good wholesale account. After all of that, you then sell your soap at half the price you would to an end consumer (retail). This is why many do not hike the path of wholesaling; but the payoffs of the initial hustle are more than worth it, for as long as your products are good and your service is exceptional, you will have a recurrent source of income over time through reorders.

When I approach a potential wholesale customer, I will often say, "I want my products to be in your store for the long haul. I want my products to be on your shelves ten years from now." And this is not just a simple sales pitch; I mean it with all of my heart, and it ensures them my focus and tenacity to make it happen. And of course when this does occur, all I have to do is answer my phone or email when the reorder comes in, put my products in a box and ship it off. Easy. Simple. Revenue.

...Or so it sounds.

Wholesaling requires you to be exceptionally organized. Operating efficiently and turning your inventory over quickly are the keys to making money when wholesaling handcrafted soap. It is a strange combination of a product/service business that deals directly with smart business customers, as opposed to the occasional naïve or inexperienced end consumer. As you are just getting your feet wet in the wholesale realm, you will quickly discover how important it is to be able to understand customer needs and quickly learn how to serve them incredibly well.

A soaping wholesaler's initial steps include defining a customer base and locating the most reliable (and most inexpensive) sources for production. These sources for production are commonly known as your "vendors" or "suppliers," which include every company that you purchase raw materials, supplies and packaging from. Your shipping/courier source should also be of careful consideration and is most certainly included as an important vendor.

Again, wholesaling is one of the purest examples of the business-to-business function, as opposed to a business-to-consumer function. If you are currently selling at craft shows, special events and through the Internet, good...keep doing that. But if the hustle and bustle of setting up, tearing down and selling a handful of bars here and there is not paying the bills, begin building your wholesale program in order to set up a recurrent stream of income over time.

Wholesale Set-up

Having the following items and functions in place for your wholesale business are essential for efficiency.

For starters, necessities like office space, a telephone, fax machine and personal computer will make up the core of your business. After many workshops, conversations at conferences and phone calls to fellow soapmakers, I was surprised to discover that not everyone has these organizational necessities in place for their company. **If you think small, your business will end**

up being small. It is a self-fulfilling prophecy. The first step towards an effective wholesale business is a rock-solid organized operation.

The next step is having the correct amount of storage and curing space for your soap and bodycare products. If you are reading this, you most likely have this in place, as you are not new to soapmaking. Keep in mind however, that you will need room to grow. If you have never wholesaled your soap before and you land four or five new accounts fairly quickly, your inventory might be depleted far faster than you planned.

You will also need dedicated space for shipping boxes, packing tape, shipping labels, packaging materials, etc. If you're delivering locally, you'll also need an appropriate and dependable vehicle. I originally had a rule of 40 miles; if one of my retail customers is located further than 40 miles from my production space, I shipped. Over time I garnered more and more wholesale clients, so I reduced the distance to 25 miles. As my business has grown, I almost solely ship to all retailers no matter the distance (unless delivered by a sales representative). Your time is money, so be careful how you spend your hours in any given day. Setting up a working relationship with one or more shipping companies like UPS, FedEx or the U.S. Postal Service will be of benefit to your business.

If all you have is the corner of your living room to work, make it work. You have to start somewhere. These considerations are certainly important and will eventually need to be put in place, but work with what you have and grow into your business space as you can. **Kitchen today, warehouse tomorrow.**

The Routine

Like many other businesses, soap wholesalers perform sales and marketing, accounting, shipping and receiving, and customer service functions on a daily basis. But unlike many kitchen crafters who sell soap through a computer screen, wholesalers have to handle tasks such as contacting existing and prospective customers, processing big orders, supporting retail buyers who need help with problems that may crop up, and performing vast amounts of market research. If, for example, you want to sell your soap in your local Whole Foods Market™, you should know every soap brand that is currently being sold in the store, their price, weight and overall branding scheme. In this example, these other sap companies are your fierce competitors, and in a franchise such as Whole Foods Market™, you will be fighting them for every inch of shelf space. Keep in mind that this is but one example; the notion of researching competition applies no matter your target customer, and we will discuss this in detail later.

To handle all of these tasks and whatever else that may come their way during the course of the day, soap wholesalers should rely on specialized software that tackles such functions as manufacturing, inventory control, shipping and receiving, accounting, client management and barcoding.

SoapMaker Professional Software

I have used SoapMaker Professional™ religiously for several years. Sure, I can figure out the cost per gram of all materials purchased, factor in tax and shipping and any discounts on an excel sheet. *But why?* Performing this tedious task after every vendor purchase of raw materials and supplies would not be the greatest use of time. SoapMaker Professional™ allows you to duplicate your raw materials/supplies purchase orders and create recipes based on what you have purchased in order to get the correct cost down to the penny. You can factor in any and all waste you might incur, per batch. You can invoice customers. You can include sales tax, which allows for easy tax remittance at the end of the month. Plus, you can keep track of inventory.

Though there are other programs out there dedicated to helping crafters come up with costs, SoapMaker Professional™ is so inherently tied to soapmaking that for my money, it is the obvious choice. My business wouldn't be the same if I didn't have this program. The only catch is, you have to take the time to put in everything you purchase that goes into your products. Only then will the costing-out of recipes be of value for you.

I still utilize QuickBooks™ for the heavy lifting of my business accounting, but I most certainly use every aspect of Soapmaker Professional™ to reduce confusion and order any raw materials or packaging that needs to be ordered.

SoapMaker Professional by Woodman Designs
[www.soapmaker.ca]

Retail Outlets, Retail Opportunities

Following is a list of different types of retail outlets. Through your own branding scheme and market research (see chapters), you can figure out what types of outlets to target for your specific products.

Department Stores

Department stores are very large stores offering a huge assortment of "soft" and "hard" goods, which often bear a resemblance to a collection of specialty stores. Such stores carry a variety of categories and they have a broad assortment of goods, usually at an average to high price. Depending on your branding scheme, department stores may be a good fit. Furthermore, department stores offer a wide variety of specialty gifts during the last quarter of the calendar year, so keep this in mind.

Discount Stores

Discount stores tend to offer a wide array of products and services, but they compete mainly on price. They offer extensive assortments of merchandise at affordable and cut-rate prices. Normally, retailers sell less fashion-oriented brands. This is not a great fit for handcrafted bodycare products.

Warehouse Stores

Warehouses stores generally offer low-cost, often high-quantity goods piled on pallets or steel shelves. Thue usually are seen as "clubs," charging an annual membership fee to members. Though this may at first sound outlandish for handcrafted bodycare products, I have seen handcrafted goods in warehouse stores on the local level.

Variety Stores

Variety stores offer extremely low-cost goods, with limited selection. This is not a great fit for handcrafted bodycare products.

Mom-And-Pop

A small retail outlet owned and operated by an individual or family. Mom and Pops focus on a relatively limited and selective set of products. These are a great fit for handcrafted bodycare products, although the volume of sales is sometimes minimal compared to other types of outlets. Mom-and-Pop stores generally engage in a lot of local-to-local business relationships, so keep this in mind on the local level.

Specialty Stores

A specialty store has a narrow marketing focus — either specializing on specific merchandise, such as toys, shoes, or clothing, or on a target audience, such as children, tourists, or oversize men. Such stores, regardless of size, tend to have a greater depth of the specialist stock than general stores, and generally offer specialist product knowledge valued by the consumer. Pricing is usually not the priority when consumers are deciding upon a specialty store; factors such as branding image, selection choice, and purchasing assistance are seen as important. They differ from department stores, which carry a wide range of merchandise. Depending on how flexible a specialty store is in bringing in new products, these can be a great fit for handcrafted bodycare products.

Concept Stores

Concept stores are similar to specialty stores. Concept stores are usually very small in size, and only ever stock one brand. They are generally run by the brand that controls them. An example of brand that distributes largely through their own widely distributed concept stores is L'OCCITANE en Provence™. Because of this, concept stores are obviously not a great fit for wholesaling handcrafted bodycare products.

General Stores

A general store is a rural store that supplies the main needs for the local community. Depending on your branding and pricing, this may or may not be a good fit for your products.

Convenience Stores

A convenience store provides limited amount of merchandise at more than average prices with a speedy checkout. This store is ideal for emergency and immediate purchases as it often works with extended hours, stocking everyday. This is not a great fit for handcrafted bodycare products.

Supermarkets

A supermarket is a self-service store consisting mainly of grocery and limited products on non-food items. Depending on your branding and pricing, this may or may not be a good fit for your products.

E-tailers

Customers shop and order through the Internet and the merchandise is dropped at their doorstep. Sometimes e-tailers use the drop-shipping technique, where they accept the payment for the product but the customer receives the product directly from the manufacturer or a wholesaler. Other times the e-tailer will actually order the product(s) from the manufacturer and ship themselves. Either way, this format is ideal for customers who do not want to travel to retail stores and are interested in home shopping.

Vending Machines

A vending machine is an automated piece of equipment wherein customers can drop money in the machine and acquire the products. Some stores take a no frills approach, while others are "mid-range" or "high end," depending on what income level they target. Before you roll your eyes at the thought, there is a lot of up and coming retailers with low budgets getting into the vending machine industry. I am currently selling soap and bodycare products in a vending machine at my local airport.

Chapter Summary

Whatever organizational ideas are sparked from reading this chapter, they will differ from soapmaker to soapmaker. The approach to organizational procedures and systems is far wider than this book's central theme. The main premise of this section is for you to think about and utilize the tools available to you, minimize time-waste and maximize production with whatever space and time you allot yourself and your business while soapmaking and selling.

— As the proprietor of a wholesale soap business, you will obviously be making soap to sell at a profit; the only difference is that you'll be working in the business-to-business realm by selling to retail companies and not to the buying public.

— Consignment is not wholesale.

— Wholesaling soap is a long-term investment and relationship.

— Establish an organized wholesaling and manufacturing set-up.

— Obtain a dedicated crafter program, such as SoapMaker Professional™.

— To make money in retail, you sell soap in **small** quantities at a **higher** price.

— To make money in wholesale, you sell soap in **large** quantities at a **lower** price.

Chapter 3

Branding / Rebranding

You enter a world of fierce competition when you begin wholesaling soap and bodycare products. Your business challengers (competitors) have everything in place, from their marketing scheme to the perfect fonts on their packaging and website. **If you already have a soap business and just simply haven't approached the wholesale market, then now is a really good time to think about who and what your business is, and whom it is serving**. The truth is that most handcrafters don't take the time or invest the money and resources to create a company brand that warrants the retail market audience.

Though genuine education is a part of the selling process in our industry, your company's branding should not only speak for itself, but also offer insight as to the drive, direction and personality of your business. Most end consumers don't know what they want until you show them. A purchasing manager in a retail outlet, however, is often well rehearsed in listening to the classic sales pitch from potential vendors. Because of this, your products, when held in the hands of a potential buyer, should immediately showcase your company's genuine, polished branding. **You could have an exceptionally good soap that smells great and lathers like a washing machine accidentally filled with dish soap, but completely lack the design, theme and polished appeal necessary to financially thrive in retail markets. This is why branding is so important in today's marketplace.**

Building a Brand

Branding is your first reference as to why your company was started in the first place. Your brand is the watermark for where your company is heading. Though branding is far more than simple design concepts, these components will accurately describe your business's character, which is what we will look at. **Remember, your branding appeal is your company's promise, purpose, walk, talk and style.**

Before we fine-tune any design components, let's back up and answer a few questions that will serve to open your mind, heart and soul as to the vivacity of your company:

1. Why does your business exist?
2. What are your company's goals?
3. What does your company stand for?
4. Describe your company's personality. Is it goofy? Or professional? Whimsical? Earthy and crunchy?

After answering the questions above (which could take some time) you now have the bird's eye view of your *business's* reasons for waking up in the morning. Now let's zoom in and answer some more specific questions:

5. Based on the insight discovered from answering the above questions, what is your company's **brand purpose** or **mission**? How will it act in agreement with what it stands for?

6. What are your company's **brand values**? Can you name at least three? These values act as a benchmark to measure your company's own performance.

7. What **promise** can you give, based on the fundamental needs of your customers?

Visual Brand Distinctions

Now it's time to get into design concepts. **This aspect is incredibly important for maintaining a cohesive visual brand, and also happens to be where most newbie soapmakers don't think things through from start to finish**. Though the list of design components could go on forever, here are the four main concepts that should be comprised by a trusted team of people, both inside and outside of your industry.

I highly recommend that you not even consider tackling these four concepts until you first answer the seven questions. In the free-form writing approach you take to answering the above questions, you might begin to visualize the brand in your mind's eye, fast-tracking the creative progress. Then zoom in on these four visual concepts:

1. Primary Logo and Proper Usage
2. Typeface (Font)
3. Color Palette
4. Photography Style (for website, catalogs, etc.)

There are vast amounts of scholarly publications about building a brand that is suited for any marketplace, so we will leave them to the brand scholars and focus on just a few concepts in this book. **Suffice it to say, in my opinion, writing, writing and more writing are the true keys to opening up the creative flow when it comes to building a brand for your business.** After you have compiled all of your answers from the seven questions, along with your jotted down ideas about the four main design components, you can begin building (or rebuilding) your perfect business brand.

Do You *Need* To Rebrand?

Your brand is the public face of your business. A well-executed rebrand can allow your company to reflect current market trends and gain a competitive advantage. Effectively rebranding allows you to sidestep your direct competition and increase your market share through an updated persona. *But do you need to?*

If you *do* need an upgrade in your business's branding, make haste. Some of the most successful businesses in the world have rebranded – several times. This can be as simple as changing your logo to completely revamping every aspect of your business, from your packaging to your website to even your mission statement.

Many times, soapmakers don't have the upfront capital required to design the perfect logo, packaging, etc. for their business. Moreover, many soapmakers haven't *put in the time* to create the perfect business brand – everything from their message, voice, tagline and values. **Many startup soapmakers have the intention to make great soap; therefore, they put all of their focus on the production and creativity of soapmaking, instead of focusing on creating a foundational corner in the market by having a unique and genuine brand appeal.** The branding of your finished soap products has to compete directly with the polished branding of the finished soap products already on the shelves of stores and shops, all the while uniquely standing out. If you are not 110 percent satisfied with the design and overall theme of your finished product, then you need to rebrand, and that's okay.

Rebranding Test Questions

1) Is Your Logo Dated?

The name and logo are the single most important design elements in your business because they are the basis for every piece of marketing and sales material your business will produce. If you are not 110 percent satisfied with your name and logo, change it. **If it isn't you, then change it into you**. Business empires like Apple™, Starbucks™ and even professional sports teams have updated their logos – multiple times – to stay trendy and fresh.

As you develop (or redevelop) your company logo, keep it simple, consistent and memorable to onlookers. The process of creating or changing your company logo should take some serious pondering and perhaps some time to develop. Hire a professional. Don't let your cousin's brother-in-law's 9-year-old niece create your logo. Come original and from the heart. **You might be in a cottage industry, but that doesn't mean you**

have to think small. Be a business owner. Think big, bold and true to you.

So, does your logo need updating? Does it currently speak to who and what your business is? Are you willing to get over the possible hurt feelings that your cousin's brother-in-law's 9-year-old niece might have if you rebrand from her old logo? Be a strong and smart business owner and recreate your brand if you feel you need to. Again, if you have even the slightest inkling to do this, then stop everything and do it.

On the top of the following page is our old logo. We wanted an *Echinacea purpurea*, commonly called purple coneflower, in our logo and branding in some way or another, as it accentuates the prairie where we live in the Midwest. This is what we came up with at the time. The faded coneflower and dated font really screams rustic and deep-rooted. Whether we liked the logo or not, we came to realize that "rustic" and "deep-rooted" were not our customer base. Our customers were young, green, and earth-conscience. This logo in no way speaks to our true customer. So we changed.

The picture below became our new logo. We wanted clean, fresh lines that offered simplicity and earthiness. And we still got our coneflower in there. We feel that this logo reflects who our customers are – minimalist by nature, earthy and natural.

In this real-life example, you can see that our logo was prohibitively dated and completely out of tune with who our true customer is. If you have really great products, perhaps even cutting-edge products, make sure your logo reflects them appropriately. Whether you create your own logo or hire a professional designer, make sure to create a logo that speaks to you and your customer with the perfect balance of simplicity and style.

2) Is Your Packaging Contemporary And Sturdy?

On the following page is a picture of a bar of our soap wrapped in our old packaging. We had our new logo, but our packaging did not warrant being on the shelves of our targeted retail outlets, such as Whole Foods Market™. In fact, one of the purchasing managers at a local Whole Foods Market™ told me this after I showed him my company's soaps. He basically conveyed that though he did like our soaps, the packaging was not good enough for their shelves. He did not say this to be insulting. In fact, it was some of the best constructive criticism that I received during sales.

And he was right. After taking a strong and realistic look at my potential competitors, I wouldn't have stood a chance. And he didn't want to pursue the product because he knew his customers better than I did. So, we had to change.

On the following page is the same soap with our new packaging. Because we knew our customer was an earth-conscience consumer, we opted for 100 percent recyclable/compostable packaging, printed with soy ink. We further accentuated the prairie with the black silhouette; after all, it is in our company's name. Additionally, we decided to package our soap in sturdy boxes because we knew we wanted our primary revenue to be wholesale, and we thought that boxes would prevent our products from being damaged by accidental drops or mishandling during shipping. Oh, and we did make our way into Whole Foods Market™ soon after our packaging change.

A Word on Packaging

In addition to wholesaling, my soap business resides in a retail shopping center as a storefront, selling not only products that we make in-house, but also local artisan goods. I love supporting local artisans and crafters, and work in conjunction with them throughout the year. However, if their packaging has not been well thought-out and is flimsy, I will not purchase their wares. As a shopkeeper, there's nothing worse than getting some lovely new product in stock, putting it out on the shelves then having to write it off a week later because the packaging rips or becomes blemished in some way at the slightest touch. It is a complete waste of money, and I've been burned on more than one occasion dealing with this issue in my store.

Thus, your packaging has to stand up to life in a store and look both extraordinary and enticing, no matter how many people have touched your soaps (and trust me, people are going to touch them!). And of course, your packaging also has to properly protect what's inside. Before we switched to our boxes, we used a cellophane shrink-wrap system. Unfortunately, the wrapping tears easily when handled by shoppers and can end up looking shoddy and damaged. That's just not good enough for retail in my opinion.

Product Photography

You can see by the difference in the old and new product pictures the sleekness and simplicity of the newer one. We use these product photos in our wholesale catalog, other print materials and website. **The quality of your product photography should most certainly be a part of your company's branding strategy.** If you can't take a great product shot, then it isn't ready to sell to the retail marketplace. And this isn't about *your* photography skills; it's about the product itself. If you do not have the wherewithal to create the perfect product photography, find someone who does.

3) Is Your Company's Name Limiting?

Your company name should be poised for expansion. Therefore, unless you have a stronghold in a local market that is not going anywhere in the next century, naming your company after locality could possibly limit your expansion capabilities later on.

Admittedly my business, Prairie Soap Company™, has a somewhat limited expansion potential based on the name. With that being said, you can find prairie in most of the United States, so it did not limit us very much at all; but I mention this so that you keep it in mind moving forward.

Though this statement certainly varies depending on your situation, I recommend staying away from names that use your city or state in them, as this can limit your expansion (Jackson County Soap Company, Wyoming Naturals, Detroit Botanicals, etc.). If you are using your locality to brand your business, really look at the implication of doing so. Is it something that can expand and grow beyond your current location? If you already have a location-based company name, do not freak out! Only you can truly know through market research how your company will fare moving forward. If you feel 100 percent confident in your company name, then by all means, don't change it!

4) Is Your Brand Distinguished?

Creating a compelling, distinguished brand means creating an emotional connection between your business and your customer. It means capturing the essence of what you do and communicating that through every decision you make for your brand.

The most important part of creating a distinguished identity is making sure that each element of your branding scheme comes together to create a powerful whole. I have seen firsthand from some soapmakers that during a branding or rebranding project, they find that many of the brand values of their company can be communicated with a specific color, as opposed to a long paragraph explaining some great attribute of the enterprise. Other times, an element or two can be showcased with newly polished appeal from a simple font change. **Everything communicates a message subconsciously and it's important that you make sure it's sending out the message you want, down to the minutest detail.**

5) Does Your Brand Appeal To Your Target Market?

Who is your customer and what do they crave? What do they do? What are their hobbies? What do they hate? Where do they shop? Where do they go for vacations? How much money do they make? How old are they?

Another way of looking at your company's brand is to look outside our industry and see what other companies do to market a specific audience. For example, Volkswagen® is not targeting the curvaceous and cute VW Bug to men 35 years and older. That's not to say there aren't any men 35 years and older cruising around in VW Bugs, but Volkswagen isn't specifically aiming at that demographic to sell their darling little compact car. A classic soap and bodycare industry example (I've seen many renditions of this) is a particular company making a woodsy, spicy, manly bar of soap. This of course is a great idea, but if the name of the company is "Super Sudsy Pink Bubbles & More," that company might not have a lot of trust built in to its targeted soap audience for that particular bar of soap. This company name example sounds more like a teenybopper audience than a lumbersexual audience. This is classic brand confusion. **Can you relate to this within your business in any way?**

When pondering your target audience, do not bottleneck your potential revenue streams too much. My latest brand, The Imperial Drifter™, is a company specifically designed for the grooming needs of men – particularly men with beards. My first inclination was to specifically target men ages 18-65. But it took only a few minutes on popular social media sites such as Pinterest™ and Instagram™ to realize that women can be just as much the driving force behind men's grooming care practices as men. This completely changed the direction I was originally going in when it came to my branding target markets. As of this writing, there have been just as many women purchasing Imperial Drifter™ products as men.

Be thoughtful and honest when answering these questions about your business. Rebranding may sound like a chore, but it will be well worth the effort

if it ultimately puts new energy into you and your business, and of course more money in your pockets!

Re-Branding Should Be Fun!

For those who dare take the unique and fun (and perhaps well-needed) chance that goes with re-branding a business, all I can say is have fun. It is a little like starting over, but more like completely re-designing an already nice home. Change out the furniture and old paintings and make your company really speak to all of the things that you love and really care for in business. This is what re-branding is all about. There is a countless amount of data out there that suggests uptick in sales and revenue in businesses being directly tied to a recent re-branding of some aspect. Take a long, hard look at your business, and if anything needs changing, now would be the time to do it.

Finally, if you can help it, don't confuse your customers by re-branding when you have already hit the wholesale scene. Start making the changes quickly so that you can play and compete in the retail outlet market in unison. If you have in fact begun the wholesaling process, yet this chapter has you thinking about change, that is okay too; companies do this all the time. Just make a plan, stick to it, get it right the first time, and then move quickly in regards to its implementation in new venues and marketing materials.

Chapter Summary

— Most handcrafters don't take the time or invest the money and resources to create a company brand that warrants the retail market audience.

— Your branding appeal is your company's promise, purpose, walk, talk and style.

— Answer the following questions as to the vivacity of your company:

1. Why does your business exist?

2. What are your company's goals?

3. What does your company stand for?

4. Describe your company's personality. Is it goofy? Or professional? Whimsical? Earthy and crunchy?

5. What is your company's **brand purpose** or **mission**? How will it act in agreement with what it stands for?

6. What are your company's **brand values**? Can you name at least three? These values act as a

benchmark to measure your company's own performance.

7. What **promise** can you give, based on the fundamental need of your customers?

— Initiate the four cornerstone design concepts:

1. Primary Logo and Proper Usage
2. Typeface (Font)
3. Color Palette
4. Photography Style (for website, catalogs, etc.)

— Answer the five rebranding test questions:

1. Is your logo dated?
2. Is your packaging contemporary and sturdy?
3. Is your company's name limiting?
4. Is your brand distinguished? Does it fill a niche?
5. Does your brand appeal to your target market?

Chapter 4

Market Research

To run a successful wholesale soap and bodycare business, you need to learn as much as possible about your customers, your competitors and our burgeoning cottage industry. **Market research is the process of probing and scrutinizing data to help you understand which soap and bodycare products are in demand, and how to be competitive within the field.**

Researching and studying our industry's trends will help you reduce risks, such as investing large sums into a trendy product that suddenly plummets in sales nationwide due to some unforeseen circumstance. Furthermore, market research will help you identify any new and upcoming sales opportunities, such as all-natural yoga mat spray or natural laundry soap.

Where To Research

Before you completely delve into the soap and bodycare wholesale business, let's first identify some outlets of information that will help you avoid costly incurrences and set you on the right track out of the gate.

The Government

The government offers an abundance of information about businesses, industries and economic conditions that can aid in conducting research. These sources provide treasured information about your customers and competitors.

According to the index of "Consumer Expenditures," at [www.bls.gov], soap and bodycare products fall under the category of "Personal Care Products And Services." Conduct a search for the latest Consumer Expenditure Report, find your category, and see if there is a percentage increase or decrease over the last few years. Study the data and comprise what you might expect the next year to be according to the trending data. This alone will help you prepare for what might come in the future as you decide to proceed in the wholesale arena.

Trades and Associations

Trade groups and associations, industry magazines and other third parties are constantly researching trends, if not creating them. Here are a few in our industry:

— **The Soap Collaborative Magazine**
www.soapcollaborative.org

— **The Handmade Cosmetic Alliance**
www.handmadecosmeticalliance.org

— **Handmade Magazine**
www.wholesalesuppliesplus.com/handmade.aspx

— **The Indie Business Network**
www.indiebusinessnetwork.org

— **The Handcrafted Soap and Cosmetic Guild**
www.soapguild.org

— **Saponifier Magazine**
www.saponifier.com

The International Marketplace

We live in a globalized marketplace. Even if you haven't sold anything out of the country, your business is still part of a globalized market, so it's important to understand the international factors that influence the soap and bodycare industry. Furthermore, it might not be that unrealistic to find an international trading partner. My first experience with this was in Canada. Though it is admittedly close by to the U.S., it was still international product trading that required a little more upfront paperwork and detailing, but ended up being a great revenue stream. These resources will help you to research potential international markets for your soap and bodycare products:

— **Market Research Guide for Exporters**
http://business.usa.gov/export/market-research/approaches-to-market-research

— **Country Market Research**
http://business.usa.gov/export-portal?tcc/Country_Market_Research/index.asp

— **BuyUSA.gov**

Product Reconnaissance

Finding a profitable niche in the already cottage, niche market that we find ourselves in as soapmakers can be a challenge. You must know what your competitors are doing and find out if you can either replicate their success or further capitalize on it by doing something that brings positive attention in a unique and different way. Reconnaissance, or the gathering of information on the ground, will provide a crystal clear picture of who your competitors are and what they are doing.

Here are 3 market reconnaissance strategies:

1) Local Market Recon

If you want to sell your soap to a local store, it's time to size up the competition that's already thriving there.

Who is your Competition?

Head into the store and have a look around:

— In your department, make a list (or take pictures on your phone) of all the soap brands on the shelves.

— How many different soap companies are represented in the store?

— Make a list of each company's prices.

— Make a list of each company's bar weight.

— Make a list of how many varieties each company is selling in the store.

   — Are the soaps being carried in the store using essential oils or synthetic fragrance oils?

   — What does the packaging look like per company?

   — What does the branding feel like per company?

When you get home, figure out the price per gram/ounce of each company. This will help you in the future when discussing pricing options with the purchasing manager. Here is an example of what it might look like to go into a store and recon the soaps and their prices:

Benjamin's Super Soaps Co.	*4 oz.*	*$4.99*
Fankie's Soaps	*3.5 oz.*	*$4.99*
Texas Soap & Thistle Co.	*5 oz.*	*$6.99*
Savon de Ayurveda Group	*4.2 oz.*	*$5.49*
Prairie Soap Company, LLC	*4 oz.*	*$7.99*
Dogwood Soaps	*3 oz.*	*$3.49*
Philadelphia Clear Soaps	*4.2 oz.*	*$5.19*
Average weight	*4 oz.*	
Average price	*$5.59*	
Average price per oz.	*$1.40*	

If this local store happens to be part of a franchise, then you can be pretty sure that these brands and prices will hold up across the selling territory of all stores. If it is an independent retail store, there might be some wiggle room in the pricing structure.

Obtaining this type of information is vital to your sales pitch and overall wholesaling efforts. If, for example, after collecting all of the information above at a local store you find that the average bar size is 3.5 oz. and you craft a 5.5 oz. bar, you might want to think about a different size, as your price might be exceedingly high compared to the competition. If all of the bars in the store are boxed or are completely wrapped and your bar is naked except for a small cigar-style band, you might want to consider different packaging. **The more you find out about your competition, the better you can equip yourself for the wholesale market.**

2) National Market Recon (via Websites)

Most often large chain stores have very up-to-date information on their websites. Very often, these websites will show you most of what they carry in their stores across the nation. This is an effective way to discover the price other soap companies are charging nationwide.

Sometimes these websites disclose the prices of products, sometimes they don't. Either way, this is a good lead into finding at least some idea of the pricing, branding schemes and bar weight of other companies.

3) Direct Market Recon

Simply jump online and start searching for soap companies that might be similar to your business in style, branding and most importantly, the targeted customer.

My business, Prairie Soap Company™, lent itself to customers who wanted a more natural lifestyle, so our branding, mission and values focused on the "natural" market very heavily. I would conduct an online search for other natural soap companies nationwide and find their "store locator" page on their websites. A vast majority of product-based businesses will show online onlookers where they are selling their products. This information is absolute gold in terms of finding like-minded businesses that are already selling like-minded products.

I would simply make a list of all the stores that they were currently selling their soap and bodycare products to. I would search dozens of websites per day and make a large master list on an excel sheet. I would then go store by store, gather all of the contact information and any other pertinent information I could about each one, and pretty soon I had a huge list of key leads that fit what my company was already selling.

As an example, if your soap company's name were something like "Suzie's Magical Baby Bubbles Soap Company," then you probably wouldn't search for natural soap companies to obtain their list of current wholesale clients. **You have to know who your customer is**. Purchasing managers at retail stores will know quickly if your soap is going to be a good fit in their store. Don't waste your time or theirs by trying to fit a square peg in a round hole. Know your customer base before you go searching for wholesale clients.

Ask Potential Buyers!

When contemplating how great your soap looks, feels, smells and performs when compared to your competition, who better to ask than your potential buyer? Approaching a purchasing manager at your local store and giving them a bar of your soap will probably not end up being a bad decision. They will love you for it, and they will also appreciate that you see them as an expert and will benefit from their honest feedback.

Compile a series of questions for them regarding your soap and make sure to get their honest opinion of your soap's packaging and branding appeal. I would also ask them who the current best selling soap company is in the store and which bar of soap is their favorite. I would then purchase a couple of bars from the competition to find out if you can experience what the purchasing manager is experiencing when he/she uses them. This is a professional and formal method of finding out what people really like. It will never hurt to get as much information as possible from professionals and direct buyers in the industry.

Your Customer & Your Competition

A wholesale business cannot succeed without understanding its customers, its products and the general market trends. In our industry, the competition becomes very fierce at the retail store level; therefore operating without conducting research will give your competitors an advantage over you.

No matter what the data you find suggests, if you are ready and willing to put in the work that wholesaling requires, you will eventually turn a profit and create success. Do not get discouraged if there is a downward trending expenditure report for the last year, or that the wholesale trade in general declined. **If you have a clear vision of success in the wholesale industry it is going to work out**. Market research is all about sizing up the competition and getting you in the right frame of mind to directly compete with the already successful soap and bodycare companies out there.

Chapter Summary

— Market research is the process of probing and scrutinizing data to help you understand which soap and bodycare products are in demand, and how to be competitive within the field.
— Where To Research:
    — The Government
    — Trades and Associations
    — The International Marketplace
— Soap and Bodycare Product Reconnaissance:
    — Local Market Recon
    — National Market Recon (via Websites)
    — Direct Market Recon
— Ask Potential Buyers!

— Wholesale businesses cannot succeed without understanding their customers, their products and general market trends. In our industry, the competition becomes very fierce at the retail store level; therefore, operating without conducting research will give your competitors an advantage over you.

Chapter 5

UPC Barcodes

"UPC" stands for Universal Product Code, which is a unique 12-digit number assigned to retail merchandise that identifies both the product and the vendor that sells the product. UPCs are regulated by GS1™, an international non-profit organization responsible for influencing and maintaining efficiency standards to meet global supply and demand. UPCs are the most commonly used retail merchandise language in the U.S. They're accompanied by an optical bit of data known as a barcode that displays a unique set of numbers and bars.

In our consumer-based society, barcodes might be one of the most recognizable languages in the world, as they are printed on virtually every consumer product around the globe. **If you want to wholesale your soap and bodycare products on a large scale, you have to have barcodes, as they are often required to be on product labels or packaging in order for the global supply chain to keep track of brands**. A barcode is simply a language used in order for the transaction cycle to take place in the most efficient way possible for retailers. They are used to encode information such as product numbers, serial numbers and batch numbers.

When a UPC barcode is scanned, it relates the product's information, whether between a manufacturer and retailer, or within its internal departments: shipping, inventory, pricing and point-of-sale (POS). For example, if a soap company sells sixteen bars of lavender soap to a retail outlet and one gets purchased (scanned at the retail outlet's cash register), the retail outlet's computer system will then deduct the bar against its inventory of that particular company's lavender bars, leaving fifteen bars in the system. Furthermore, if a customer wasn't sure of the price of the bar, a store representative can simply scan the barcode to find out how much it costs, as this data would have been entered into the system by the purchasing manager before the product went out on the selling floor.

The UPC was originally developed for the grocery industry, but has since spread to almost all areas of retail business. UPC barcodes not only make it easy to identify products, they allow retailers to program their POS systems with prices and other necessary information for each product.

Understanding a UPC

UPCs do not carry prices in and of themselves. When scanned, the UPC identifies the product and will pull up the price. The price however, is entered by the retailer and put into their POS (Point of Sale) system. **Therefore, based on the price that you and the retailer have agreed upon during the sale, the retailer will then enter the price of the product for his/her store.**

Each variety of soap and/or bodycare products you make and wholesale will have its own UPC. Your lavender soap, herbs soap and coffee scrub will all have different UPCs, even though the same company makes them all.

Obtaining Barcodes

To acquire UPC barcodes, you first must obtain a unique GS1 Company Prefix by joining GS1™. After paying an initial fee and an annual maintenance fee, you will have access to up to 100 UPC codes.

Visit http://www.gs1.org/barcodes/implementation for all of the information you will need.

Not All Barcodes Are Created Equal

Not all UPC barcodes are created equal. There are many internet-based companies who offer UPCs and claim that their barcodes originate from GS1™, thus making them official; however, many are not. **Only GS1™ can give your company a single, unique company prefix number that will only be used by your company**. The company prefix is a unique identifier, which represents *one* particular company. If you were to purchase a UPC from one of those internet-based "resellers," you would only be receiving a single UPC number whose company prefix might or might not be currently assigned to another company. This obviously can create massive confusion if a retail outlet happens to purchase items from two completely different vendors who have the same UPC barcode for a product.

Because of this deceitful practice (there have been court cases settling in the multi-millions due to this misconduct) from many new UPC "resellers," most reputable retailers now have a policy wherein they only accept UPC barcodes that are directly assigned from GS1™.

There *are* companies you can obtain UPC barcodes from that will give you a unique company prefix. If you do end up purchasing a UPC from a reseller, you better have confidence in that reseller to assign unique UPC numbers. How can you be sure that the number assigned has not already been sold to someone else? If you do decide to work with a reseller, make sure you feel comfortable with the legitimacy and security of the company you choose. That said, you will know with complete confidence that you are obtaining a unique prefix if you just go through GS1™ from the start, so I strongly advise you to do so.

Steps to Assigning a UPC Barcode

After you have signed up and paid the initial fee, GS1™ will have assigned you a unique company prefix number, along with a username and password to an online portal, called "Data Driver®."

As you can see, my business, Prairie Soap Company™, was issued a company prefix of 085410002. **This means that for every UPC barcode I create for each one of my products, the first 9 digits of each UPC barcode number will be this prefix.**

Data Driver® is an online tool from GS1™ that helps you identify your products and create barcodes. You can create your own UPC barcodes through GS1™,

but why do that when Data Driver® can do it for you?
All you have to do is put in a few pieces of necessary data
about your product and it does the rest.

Products

Identify your products with Global Trade Item Numbers (GTINs) including U.P.C.s. Capture that information in barcodes that may be printed or downloaded. Share your product information with your trading partners by creating Sales Sheets.

Available Options

[Assign a GTIN to a Product] [Assign a GTIN to a Variable Measure Product]

⊟ Search My Entered Items

Items matching your criteria 104 of 104

[Edit] [Clone] [Summary] [Product Sales Sheet] [Print Barcode]

Search Tips

Status	For Re-Use Date	Level	Brand Name	Description	SKU	GTIN-14	GTIN-12 (U.P.C.)	Prefix
In Use		Each	The Imperial Drifter	Beard Balm - Trailhead		00854100002927	854100002927	854100002
In Use		Each	The Imperial Drifter	Beard Balm - Black Spruce		00854100002910	854100002910	854100002
In Use		Each	The Imperial Drifter	Beard Balm - Clary Sage		00854100002903	854100002903	854100002
In Use		Each	The Imperial Drifter	Beard Balm - Juniper Berry		00854100002897	854100002897	854100002
In Use		Each	The Imperial Drifter	Beard Oil - Clary Sage		00854100002880	854100002880	854100002
In Use		Each	The Imperial Drifter	Beard Oil - Juniper Berry		00854100002873	854100002873	854100002
In Use		Each	The Imperial Drifter	Beard Oil - Trailhead		00854100002866	854100002866	854100002
In Use		Each	The Imperial Drifter	Beard Oil - Black Spruce		00854100002859	854100002859	854100002
In Use		Each	Project Lydia	Elephant Print Handbags		00854100002842	854100002842	854100002
In Use		Each	Prairie Soap Company	Premium Peppermint Aftershave	10221	00854100002835	854100002835	854100002
In Use		Each	Prairie Soap Company	Peppermint Shave Soap Travel	10220	00854100002828	854100002828	854100002
In Use		Each	Prairie Soap Company	Peppermint Shave Soap	10219	00854100002811	854100002811	854100002
In Use		Each	Prairie Soap Company	Premium Shave Set	10218	00854100002804	854100002804	854100002
In Use		Each	Prairie Soap Company	Gritty Gardener's Hand Kit	10217	00854100002798	854100002798	854100002
In Use		Each	Prairie Soap Company	Prairie Fresh Lotion	10102	00854100002781	854100002781	854100002
In Use		Each	Prairie Soap Company	Lip Balm Rosemary & Lime		00854100002774	854100002774	854100002
In Use		Each	Prairie Soap Company	Lip Balm Peppermint		00854100002767	854100002767	854100002
In Use		Each	Prairie Soap Company	Whipped Shea Butter - Lavender, Clove & Ylang Ylang	10119	00854100002750	854100002750	854100002
In Use		Each	Prairie Soap Company	Whipped Shea Butter - Cedarwood & Fir Needle	10118	00854100002743	854100002743	854100002
In Use		Each	Prairie Soap Company	Whipped Shea Butter - Tea Tree	10180	00854100002736	854100002736	854100002
In Use		Each	Prairie Soap Company	Whipped Shea Butter - Lavender Lemon	10117	00854100002729	854100002729	854100002
In Use		Inner pack	Prairie Soap Company	Mint Grapefruit - 8 Pack	10009	10854100002412	N/A	854100002

The picture on the previous page is a screen shot of the "products" page from my company's Data Driver® portal. You can see both of my company's brands, *Prairie Soap Company, LLC*™ and *The Imperial Drifter* ™. In order to better understand the column headers, let's walk through creating a new soap that will be sold to major retail outlets.

Step 1:

On the main Products page, click the tab "Assign a GTIN to a Product".

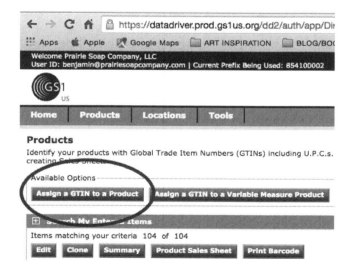

Step 2:

Assign the appropriate "packaging level." We are creating one product (one variety of soap); therefore, we will be selling at the "each" level. The "each" level is the lowest level of item packaging. These units are almost always sold at the point-of-sale. This typically is the product by itself, and will almost always be the case for selling soap to retail outlets.

| Home | Products | Locations | Tools |

Packaging Level

Products are packaged at different levels, and each level requires a specific type of barcode. Choose the option below that best describes your packaging for your product:

Note: Packaging levels are hierarchical, which means you must define the lowest level (each/individual unit) first before proceeding to a higher level.

Please select the option below that best describes the packaging level you want to barcode.

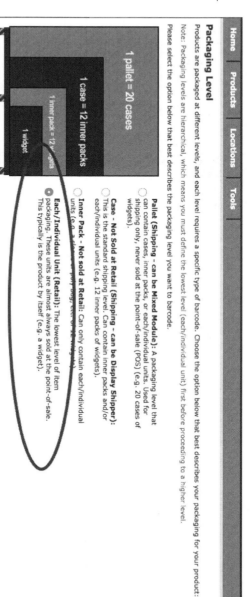

1 pallet = 20 cases

1 case = 12 inner packs

1 inner pack = 12 widgets

1 widget

○ **Pallet (Shipping - can be Mixed Module):** A packaging level that can contain cases, inner packs, or each/individual units. Used for shipping only, never sold at the point-of-sale (POS) (e.g. 20 cases of widgets).

○ **Case - Not Sold at Retail (Shipping - can be Display Shipper):** This is the standard shipping level. Can contain inner packs and/or each/individual units (e.g. 12 inner packs of widgets).

○ **Inner Pack - Not sold at Retail:** Can only contain each/individual units (e.g. a ~~12 pack of pouches~~ ~~or single packs~~).

◉ **Each/Individual Unit (Retail):** The lowest level of item packaging. These units are almost always sold at the point-of-sale. This typically is the product by itself (e.g. a widget).

Step 3:

On the next page, you will fill out the "Product Details." The first field required is the *Brand Name*. This will be your company's name. The next field required is the *Primary Product Description*. This will be the name of your new product. Although you are only required to fill out the first two fields, you may fill out the rest, which include an internal part number and your products' measurements.

NEW PRODUCT: Product Details

* Denotes a mandatory field

Product Identification

Brand Name * | Prairie Soap Company, LLC

Primary Product Description * | Luxury Unscented Bar

Internal Part Number or SKU

Status* | In Use ◇

Product Measurements (Optional)

Dimensions

Height	Width	Depth	Measurement Unit
			Select One ◇

Weights

Gross Weight	Net Weight	Measurement Unit
		Select One ◇

Benjamin D. Aaron

Step 4:

Verify that everything on the screen is correct. You may go back to edit any field at this point before saving the product. GS1 has now generated a 12-digit UPC for your new product. Along with the actual barcode itself, this number will be on your products' packaging.

91

Step 5:

Now we have an assigned UPC for our product. The next step is to either print them or deliver them to a designer in a format compatible with design software. Make sure the correct product is highlighted in the far left column and then select the "Print Barcode" button. See the following page.

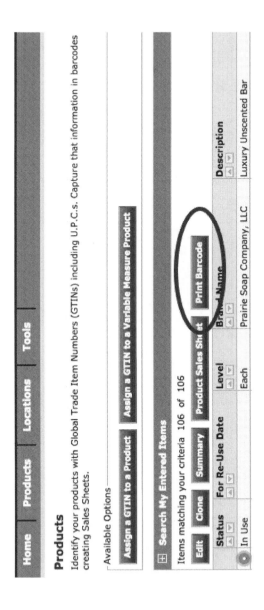

Step 6:

On the "Print Product Barcode" page, we can select which size barcode dimensions we would like to print. There are five sizes, all of which will work perfectly fine for small soap bar packaging. I always chose the smallest size so that my packaging had adequate space for everything else. See the following page.

Print Product Barcode

Select a Barcode to Print. If you need help with your selections, work with your trading partner, refer to the _GS1 General Specifications_ or contact Member

Your Product

Brand Name:	Prairie Soap Company, LLC	**GTIN-14:**	00854100002934
Product Description:	Luxury Unscented Bar	**GTIN-12 (U.P.C.):**	854100002934
Internal Part Number or SKU:			
Product Dimensions:			

Select a Barcode to Print

Barcode Type   UPC-A ◇

Application Area   Packages/Containers Scanned in General Retail at POS ◇

Barcode Dimensions ✓ Smallest W 1.175 X H 0.817 (inches)
     Small W 1.322 X H 0.919 (inches)
     Recommended W 1.469 X H 1.021 (inches)
     Large W 2.204 X H 1.531 (inches)
     Largest W 2.938 X H 2.042 (inches)

This is considered an 80% (10.4 mil) U.PC and it is specified as the smallest U.PC that will scan consistently.

Step 7:

Whether you are printing your barcode or not, coming this far in the steps is required so that you may at least download the UPC barcode file. This step gives you two file format options:

PNG (.png) File

A PNG, or Portable Network Graphics file, is a raster graphics file format that supports lossless data compression.

EPS (.eps) File

An EPS, or Encapsulated Postscript, is a file extension for a graphics file format used in vector-based images in Adobe Illustrator. Thus, if you were working with a designer (or want to tackle the design job yourself) to create your packaging, you would download the UPC barcode as an EPS file and then send it to him/her. See the following page.

Print Barcode

Print your barcode directly to a predetermined set of standard labels or download the barcode image for printing externally. You may also contact GS1 US

Your Product

Brand Name: Prairie Soap Company, LLC

Product Description: Luxury Unscented Bar

Internal Part Number or SKU:

Product Dimensions:

GTIN-14: 00854100002934

GTIN-12 (U.P.C.): 85410002934

Barcode Print Specifications

Barcode Type: UPC-A

Application Area: Packages/Containers Scanned in General Retail at POS

Barcode Dimensions: Smallest W 1.175 X H 0.817 (Inches)

Download Image or Print barcode labels

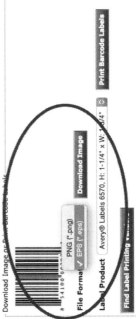

File Format: ✓ EPS (*.eps) | PNG (*.png)

Download Image

Label Product: Avery® Labels 6570, H: 1-1/4" x W: 1-3/4" ◇

Find Label Printing Vendors

Print Barcode Labels

Another option from this page is to choose between two "Label Product" templates that GS1™ has comprised in conjunction with Avery™. If you choose to print yourself and use one of these options, you will be instructed to set your printer page margins specifically to the template labels you choose to purchase from Avery™. Though this is convenient, you are left with a rather large sticker that you then have to place on your already packaged bar of soap. If you are going to go through the lengths of obtaining a company prefix and developing a series of UPC barcodes for your products, I would recommend your packaging be designed and printed in bulk, which would warrant you downloading each UPC barcode as an EPS and handing them off to your designer to utilize in the design.

So in about seven steps you can create a UPC barcode that is unique to your company and your product. The best part is you can "clone" each product you create in Data Driver® if you so choose, only changing out the "Product Description" field (the name of the product) for a quick and efficient method to making a line of different soap varieties.

Completed UPC Barcode using Data Driver®

Each variety of soap you sell will require a barcode. Each variety of lip balm. Each variety of body scrub, etc. For example, you would need 20 barcodes if your wholesale product lineup looked like this:

— 8 varieties of soap
— 8 varieties of lip balm
— 4 varieties of body scrub

Designing with UPC Barcodes

Once you have generated UPC barcodes for each product in your line, the next step is to utilize them in your packaging. Remember that your designer will most likely use the EPS file format in their design work. Though it isn't required, most UPC barcodes do best against a white background. Also, your designer may need to shrink the UPC barcode image in order to make it fit on the packaging. This is usually okay, but too much shrinking can cause problems when scanned at a store register.

What is generally advised is to cut off some of the top of the code as opposed to actually shrinking the image down. This keeps the black and white spaces the same from left to right; it just gives it a haircut, so to speak. Never cut off the numbers on the bottom of each barcode.

Full-Sized UPC Barcode, Uncropped

Cropping the top of the UPC Barcode in order to shrink the size without disrupting the pattern of black lines and white spaces, left to right.

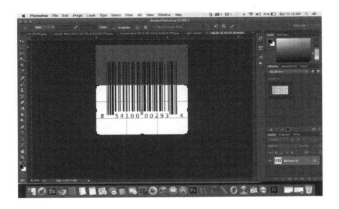

Obtaining UPC barcodes is neither complicated nor expensive. It is simply part of the cost of production in the business-to-business structure that we find ourselves in as wholesalers. There are several companies you can obtain UPC barcodes from, and I personally am not in the know about most. What I can tell you however, is that obtaining your company prefix and UPC barcodes from GS1™ is the safest and most assured way to your barcoding endeavors. Data Driver® is an easy online tool within the GS1™ site that allows for easy organization and quick UPC barcode generation. If you are new to the idea of UPC barcodes, rest assured that obtaining them and implementing them is much easier than you may have first realized.

Chapter Summary

— If you want to wholesale your soap and bodycare products on a large scale, you have to have barcodes, as they are generally required to be on product labels or packaging in order for the global supply chain to keep track of brands.

— UPCs are regulated by GS1™, an international non-profit organization responsible for influencing and maintaining efficiency standards to meet global supply and demand.

— Understanding a UPC:

  — UPCs do not carry prices in and of themselves. The retailer enters the price of the product.

  — Each variety of soap and/or bodycare products you make and wholesale will have its own UPC.

  — Not all barcodes are created equal.

  — Only GS1™ can give your company a single, unique company prefix number that will only be used by your company.

— Incorporating UPC barcodes in packaging design:

  — Your designer will most likely use the EPS file format in their design work.

  — Though it isn't required, most UPC barcodes do best against a white background.

  — Your designer may need to shrink the UPC barcode image in order to make it fit on the packaging. This is usually okay, but too much shrinking can cause problems when scanned at the register.

Please keep in mind…

These step-by-step instructions with accompanying screenshots will most likely be outdated in a few years due to the recurrent updates that websites perform; however, I can say that little has changed in the nine years I have been utilizing GS1™ and its online portal, Data Driver®. Though the online portal might change a bit, the overall step-by-step functioning will most likely stay very similar.

Chapter 6

Know Your Costs
Know Your Price

I've seen many soapers begin the wholesaling process
without a firm understanding of their true costs to
produce a bar of soap. This is like entering a foot race
with two broken legs. You will work far too hard for far
too little if your pricing is not exactly as it should be.

Unfortunately, in the soaping world, the **market
value** of soap has been somewhat set by the very large,
commercial bar soap companies. Though the tide is
shifting in the public's pricing awareness with handmade
soap, the fact is that a lot of time and labor goes into
handcrafting soap, and the margins just aren't that great
because of the *value perception* implied by the synthetic

detergent bars on the market. Therefore, if you sell your bar of soap at a wholesale price that is even 10 cents less than it should be, your company will suffer greatly. **Every penny counts when it comes to wholesaling.**

Value Perception

Value perception can be defined as the worth that a product has in the mind of the consumer. The consumer's perceived value of a product affects the price that he or she is willing to pay.

A great example of value perception is perfumes. Perfumes and colognes tend to be associated with a glamorous celebrity in order to create a mystique and perception of luxury. Alternatively, they may be the subjects of elaborate and expensive advertising campaigns to create a strong image for the perfume. Consumers commonly do not realize that the costs of production for perfumes are extremely low. Thus, while the cost of production for perfume may be only a few dollars, the perceived value of a perfume can be far greater—some with a price range far exceeding three digits and even four digits. Can you think of some products in our industry that has relatively low production cost with high-perceived value?

Thus, for the most part, consumers are unaware of the true cost of production for the products they buy. Instead, they simply have an internal feeling for how much products are worth to them. As is the case within our industry, giant corporations like Procter & Gamble™ and Unilever™ have created a value perception of a bar of soap that is much less than what we handcrafters can sell our soap at. Thus, in order to obtain a higher price for our products, we must pursue marketing and branding strategies to create a higher perceived value for our products. But, branding and marketing is not this chapter's premise; **though we must of course create an incredible branding scheme to compete in the marketplace, everything comes down to cost. The more economical you can make your bar of soap, the more you can compete. So let's talk more about cost.**

Cost Per Unit Of Measure

If you don't currently have SoapMaker Professional™ or another software program that tracks your material costs, purchases, postage, and labor such as CraftyBase™

(www.craftybase.com), now would be a good time to obtain one. If you do have a program, input every single raw material you buy along with any tax and shipping costs you might incur. Then create your recipe with the cost of packaging, materials and anything else, down to the minutest detail. This will create your truest cost per bar in the fastest and easiest way possible.

Whether you have software or not, provided is an example of all the costs that might go into a batch of soap. Please keep in mind that this is a mere example, and should not be taken as the way in which to proceed in ordering your raw materials.

Below is a bar of soap that we will call "The Famous Luxury Unscented Bar." Let's take a look at the recipe:

Ingredients	Quantity
Olive Oil	18 oz.
Coconut Oil	18 oz.
Almond Oil	5 oz.
Avocado Oil	5 oz.
Rice Bran Oil	5 oz.
Shea Butter	5 oz.
Castor Oil	4 oz.
NaOH	8.4 oz.
Yield:	20 Bars

Below are the purchase orders for the raw materials:

PO from "Super Duper Oils & Butters Co."

Item	Weight	Cost
Olive Oil	35 lbs.	$90.00
Coconut Oil	50 lbs.	$65.00
Almond Oil	35 lbs.	$105.00
Avocado Oil	35 lbs.	$125.00
Rice Bran Oil	35 lbs.	$60.00
Shea Butter	25 lbs.	$75.00
Castor Oil	35 lbs.	$74.00
Shipping		$90.00

PO from "Essential Lye Station Co."

Item	Weight	Cost
NaOH	128 lbs.	$180.00
Shipping		$100.00

All of the ingredients for the "The Famous Luxury Unscented Bar" recipe are in pounds. This is generally the case when ordering from suppliers. Let's break down all of the ingredients from both POs (Purchase Orders) into ounces by multiplying the pounds purchased by 16 (16 ounces per pound):

PO from "Super Duper Oils & Butters Co."

Item	Weight (x16)	Ounces	Cost
Olive Oil	35 lbs.	560	$90.00
Coconut Oil	50 lbs.	800	$65.00
Almond Oil	35 lbs.	560	$105.00
Avocado Oil	35 lbs.	560	$125.00
Rice Bran Oil	35 lbs.	560	$60.00
Shea Butter	25 lbs.	400	$75.00
Castor Oil	35 lbs.	560	$74.00
Shipping			$90.00

PO from "Essential Lye Station Co."

Item	Weight (x16)	Ounces	Cost
NaOH	128 lbs.	2,048	$180.00
Shipping			$100.00

The shipping cost for all the oils and butters purchased totals $90. The total weight for this purchase is 4,000 oz. Since we know the total amount of shipping weight and shipping charge, we can now figure out how much to charge each item, based on the amount purchased in ounces. Each item's weight is a fraction, or percentage, of the total weight of the shipment (4,000 oz). For example, the amount of olive oil purchased was 560 oz. out of 4,000. 560/4,000 = 0.14. The weight of the olive oil represents 0.14, or 14% of the total weight of the purchase. Let's see what the rest of the oils and butters look like:

PO from "Super Duper Oils & Butters Co."

Item	Ounces	Calculation	%
Olive Oil	560	560/4,000=.14	14%
Coconut Oil	800	800/4,000=.20	20%
Almond Oil	560	560/4,000=.14	14%
Avocado Oil	560	560/4,000=.14	14%
Rice Bran Oil	560	560/4,000=.14	14%
Shea Butter	400	400/4,000=.10	10%
Castor Oil	560	560/4,000=.14	14%
Total	4,000		100%

Now that we know the fraction, or percentage of weight of each ingredient purchased, we can take each and multiply by the total shipping cost, which is $90.

PO from "Super Duper Oils & Butters Co."

Item	%	Total PO Shipping	Per Item Shipping Cost
Olive Oil	14%		$12.60
Coconut Oil	20%		$18.00
Almond Oil	14%		$12.60
Avocado Oil	14%		$12.60
Rice Bran Oil	14%		$12.60
Shea Butter	10%		$9.00
Castor Oil	14%		$12.60
Total	100%	$90.00	$90.00

Now we simply add the shipping cost per item to the original amount charged, per item:

PO from "Super Duper Oils & Butters Co."

Item	Cost	Per Item Shipping Cost	Total Item Cost
Olive Oil	$90.00	$12.60	$102.60
Coconut Oil	$65.00	$18.00	$83.00
Almond Oil	$105.00	$12.60	$117.60
Avocado Oil	$125.00	$12.60	$137.60
Rice Bran Oil	$60.00	$12.60	$72.60
Shea Butter	$75.00	$9.00	$84.00
Castor Oil	$74.00	$12.60	$85.60

We have the true cost, per ingredient. Now let's divide the total by the amount of ounces.

PO from "Super Duper Oils & Butters Co."

Item	Total Item Cost	Ounces	True Cost Per Ounce
Olive Oil	$102.60	560	$0.18
Coconut Oil	$83.00	800	$0.10
Almond Oil	$117.60	560	$0.21
Avocado Oil	$137.60	560	$0.25
Rice Bran Oil	$72.60	560	$0.13
Shea Butter	$84.00	400	$0.21
Castor Oil	$85.60	560	$0.15

The far right column gives the true cost per ingredient. This will be implemented into the recipe to give us our most specific cost per batch of soap. Following the same process used to figure the true cost per ounce per oil, the NaOH true cost per ounce ends up being $0.14/oz.

Now it is time to plug these numbers into the "Famous Luxury Unscented Bar" to figure out our cost per bar. This recipe makes 20 bars of soap.

Ingredients	Quantity	True Cost Per Ounce	Recipe Total
Olive Oil	18 oz.	$0.18	$3.24
Coconut Oil	18 oz.	$0.10	$1.80
Almond Oil	5 oz.	$0.21	$1.05
Avocado Oil	5 oz.	$0.25	$1.25
Rice Bran Oil	5 oz.	$0.13	$0.65
Shea Butter	5 oz.	$0.21	$1.05
Castor Oil	4 oz.	$0.15	$0.60
NaOH	8.4 oz.	$0.14	$1.18
	Total Materials Cost		$10.82

Now that we have the true cost of the batch in raw materials, we can now add the cost of packaging. Here is the example PO from your packaging source:

PO from "Soapy Package Plus Co."

Item	Units	Cost Per Unit	Cost
Printed Soap Box	5,000	$0.15	$750.00
Shipping			$50.00

Following the same process used to figure the true cost per ounce per oil, the packaging true cost per box ends up being $0.16/box.

Now let's combine all materials and packaging costs, down to the penny. This batch makes 20 bars so we'll need 20 soapboxes for packaging.

Ingredients	Quantity	True Cost Per Unit	Recipe Total
Olive Oil	18 oz.	$0.18	$3.24
Coconut Oil	18 oz.	$0.10	$1.80
Almond Oil	5 oz.	$0.21	$1.05
Avocado Oil	5 oz.	$0.25	$1.25
Rice Bran Oil	5 oz.	$0.13	$0.65
Shea Butter	5 oz.	$0.21	$1.05
Castor Oil	4 oz.	$0.15	$0.60
NaOH	8.4 oz.	$0.14	$1.18
Soap Box	20 pieces	$0.16	$3.20
		Total Materials Cost	**$14.02**

Labor

This particular recipe example makes 20 bars of soap. For the soapmaking veteran, this batch would most likely take an hour to complete, including the cutting of the soap the following day, placing the bars on a curing rack and later packaging each bar.

So What Is My Hourly Wage?

Well, what do you want it to be?! There isn't one established method or formula for coming up with labor costs per batch of soap. Why? Because creating a wage is so subjective to an individual business. This method is effective in getting a close number to labor, but you should come up with your own methodology and do it quickly before you realize you aren't charging enough for the soap and bodycare products you are already selling. With that being said, we can at least get a baseline in order to find the true cost of "The Famous Luxury Unscented Bar."

Let's say you would like to earn $25 per hour from your business. If you are the only one making this particular batch of soap from start to finish and it takes one hour to complete, your manufacture costs for this batch look like this:

Cost of Production, 20 Bars

Item	Amount
Materials Cost	$14.02
Labor Cost	$25.00
Total Manufacturing Cost	$39.02

Labor Cost: A Quick and Easy Method.

You can create your labor costs however you want; you are the business owner. But here is a quick, down-and-dirty method to finding out how much you are currently worth to your business in dollar amounts.

—Add up the amount you made in sales from the last month.

—Count up how many items you sold to make that amount of money.

—Work out the manufacturing cost (materials and packaging only) of making that number of items.

—Work out your monthly total for all overheads.

—Add your manufacturing costs (materials and packaging) for the items you sold to your monthly overheads. Then subtract this figure from the amount you made in sales. **This shows how much was left over once your costs are taken care of.**

—Now work out how many hours you spent on your business last month. Take the figure for left over money and divide it by the number of hours you worked.

This figure is your current hourly rate. Does it need improvement?

What is Overhead?

Overhead costs are extremely individual and specific to a particular business. You really have to do your homework to find out what additional costs you have outside of materials and labor. This could be accounting costs, newsletter subscriber fees, site hosting fees, basic office supplies, travel costs, site design fees, giveaways, donations, rent/utilities and much more. **How you factor in the overhead costs of your business is entirely up to you.**

Whatever costs you incur over the course of the year, break everything down into monthly expenses. Once you have all of your expenses broken down by the month, how can you cover them? Will you include a fraction of your overhead costs with each product you list, or will you focus on reaching a specific sales goal in order to cover your overhead costs? In my business, we do the latter. We make specific sales goals each month that we know will cover the cost of overhead, labor and materials. However you approach it, make a plan and write it down.

Cost of Production, 20 Bars

Item	Amount
Materials Cost	$14.02
Labor Cost	$25.00
Total Manufacturing Cost	**$39.02**
$39.02 / 20 bars = $1.95	

As you can see in our example, it is costing the business $1.95 in materials and labor to produce "The Famous Luxury Unscented Bar." If you feel comfortable in knowing all your overhead costs per month, you can incorporate that cost into each bar of soap and make a projection of sales that will cover it.

The Markup

Once you have the base production cost of one bar, you can now determine what sort of markup you would like to add to your soap. **A markup is defined as the amount added to your cost price to arrive at a selling price and is a commonly used technique in determining how much to charge for your products.**

Markups are classically defined as a percentage. A markup of 100 percent would be your total manufacturing cost (of one product) x 2. For example, if Sue makes a body scrub that costs $2.25 in total manufacturing costs and then adds a markup of 100 percent, the markup percentage results in $4.50. With the **value perception** of body scrubs being what they are in the current marketplace, Sue would be shooting herself in the foot with this markup. In reality, the markup percentage on a bodycare product such as a scrub should be more in the ballpark of 700 percent or more. A 700 percent markup would bring the body scrub to $18, which is more than fair for a handmade scrub.

It is important that you understand the difference between a **percentage markup** and a **profit margin**. The above example demonstrates a 700 percent markup, not a 700 percent profit margin. The profit margin in the body scrub example is $15.75.

Profit – Total Manufacturing Cost = Profit Margin
$18.00 - $2.25 = $15.75

Therefore, the **profit margin percentage** for the body scrub is 87.5 percent, which is an incredible profit margin in the handmade bodycare industry.

Profit Margin / Profit = Profit Margin Percentage
$15.75 / $18.00 = 0.875 (87.5%)

Alas, the market value perception of *soap* will not allow for this type of profitable markup. As previously stated, the market value of soap has been somewhat set by the very large, commercial bar soap companies.

Though the tide is shifting in the public's pricing awareness with handmade soap, the fact is that a lot of labor and material costs go into handcrafting soap, and the profit margins do not reflect this because of the current *value perception* put forth by the synthetic detergent bars on the market. **Due to this marketplace circumstance, a markup of 100 percent is probably all you will be able to get away with, but by all means, if you can do more, then do so.**

Total Manufacturing Cost x 2 = Wholesale Price

In the "Famous Luxury Unscented Bar" example, our cost and markup looks like this:

$$\$1.95 \times 2 = \$3.90$$

This scenario would suggest that purchasing managers would order your soap at the wholesale price of $3.90 per bar.

SRP and the Keystone Markup

Purchasing managers are going to want you to tell them at what price they should sell your bar of soap. This is the suggested retail price, or SRP. Traditionally, retailers always strive for the "keystone" markup, which is simply double the amount you charge them per bar (100 percent). In the "Famous Luxury Unscented Bar" example (wholesale price of $3.90), this would follow that a purchasing manager would ideally want to sell your soap in their store at $7.79 per bar. In my opinion, this is just **on the brink of being priced too high, depending on your targeted retailer**. I've heard on many occasions from folks in our industry who suggest that there are more than enough markets out there that will sell your soap at $9 - $12 per bar. This may be true. Who am I to say otherwise? Admittedly, I haven't investigated every retail store out there in the marketplace.

However, I do think that this is a flawed approach to selling wholesale on a large and recurrent scale. Though I love the optimism, I just simply don't agree with the premise that there are enough retailers out there willing to purchase at high prices ($5.00 or more wholesale) and realistically expect revenue sustainability for soap that is priced that high. Wholesaling soap is about reorders. And reorders. And reorders. If you price your soap in the $5 wholesale price range, your purchasing managers are forced to raise the price extremely high compared to many on the market. And don't get me wrong; there are plenty of retailers out there who will make *initial* purchases for this price. In fact, selling to retailers at these prices might not be all that difficult – but *their* customers are the end consumers. It is ultimately up to *them*. When middle to upper middle class folks see $9-$12 for a bar of soap, they immediately think "super-specialized" and "gifty." Again, this is completely fine if this is indeed your niche in the market – don't let me sway you otherwise. If you can pull it off, than do it!

However, pricing this high puts the "artisan boutique" stamp extremely high in the eyes of consumers. Once your soap has the perception of being "artisan boutique," your soap can become a little too special – it becomes an idea for birthday and holiday gifts, or a nice rustic perfume block that never actually gets used by anyone.

This might work for the last quarter of the year, but it won't have staying power; the price might dramatically slow down sales over the course of the calendar year. I have seen this first hand by my very favorite (and a very prominent) soap company. Their price point for bar soap became too high for the market to bear, so they eventually just stopped making bar soap and switched to liquid soap, as the margins are better. They literally priced their bar soaps out of the market. Now they occasionally make them for the last quarter of the year, as the bar soaps are almost strictly seen as super-specialized and gifty.

My Pricing Disclaimer

I **never** want to deter you from pricing your bars as high as you possibly can. My experience has led me to the above explanation, and your situation might *certainly be different. My company sells to a variety of health market chain stores across the country, thus my vantage point is expressed through this circumstance. Your job is to do your research and homework to discover what your targeted market will bear for your products.*

Let's Try This Again

All things considered, are your soaps and bodycare products valued commodities that will warrant repeat purchases, or are they a special, niche gift? Your price and your customer ultimately determine this. Selling at the right price to retail outlets is the perfect balance between high-value and reasonable price. According to the Harvard Business School, we Americans, on average, buy the same 150 products over and over. The data compiled suggests that these same 150 products make up about 85 percent of our household needs. So, the question is, how do you infiltrate the minds of consumers and create a habit-forming circumstance so they purchase your soap? And re-purchase? And re-purchase? The answer? A quality product at a reasonable price.

Lowering Costs

Based on the pricing concepts above, the "Famous Luxury Unscented Bar" might be costing us too much to manufacture. Thus, we discernibly need to lower the cost of manufacturing. There are two simple and direct ways to lowering costs:

1) Economy of Scale

When more units of soap are produced on a larger scale and done so at a lower-than-previous cost, economies of scale have been reached. Let's examine how we do this:

— Lower Material Costs

When a company buys inputs in bulk, it can take advantage of volume discounts. McDonald's isn't buying potatoes to turn into French fries at the local grocery store. They are purchasing in extremely large volumes. Thus, if you really want to get your costs down, this is the first obvious step. Taking the step from 50 lb. pails of base oils to 420 lb. drums will significantly drop the price of your soap. This will obviously be a bigger cost incurrence upfront, but will significantly drop the price of your soap per ounce.

— Specialized Equipment

As the scale of production of a company increases, a company can employ the use of better equipment resulting in greater efficiency. The "Famous Luxury Unscented Bar" example yields 20 bars of soap. If you are serious about wholesaling, it is time to scale up. Depending on the amount of wholesale customers you want to have, and the amount (and variety) of units you will sell, having a system in place that yields 100 – 200 bars of soap per batch will decrease labor costs and make things easier and more efficient.

A Word About Soap Equipment

Maximizing your production while reducing labor costs is a big hurdle for folks in our industry. If you have a savings system in place for the revenue you generate through your business, I would urge you to save up for bigger and better equipment whenever you can. I know there are several equipment companies out there who cater to our handcrafted, up-scaling needs in regards to bigger production equipment, but I have only dealt with one, Soap Equipment. Based on my experience with Soap Equipment's customer service and quality of equipment, I would highly recommend them (www.soapequipment.com).

2) If Needed, Change Your Recipe

Gasp! I realize this might strike a negative chord with you! How dare I suggest you change your perfect, unique recipe?!?!

If you are going to make it in the wholesale arena as a handcrafter, you are going to need to really look at your costs. One of the most obvious cost-cutters is to create a line of soaps that are made with less expensive materials. This doesn't mean you have to stop making soap with babassu and meadowfoam seed oils, I am simply suggesting that you make a small line of soaps that are of good quality, unique, yet affordable. **The economic feasibility of your product line depends on its affordability to the retail outlet, and ultimately their customers.**

Let's try a different, simpler recipe. First, we need to purchase oils.

PO from "Super Duper Oils & Butters Co."

Item	Weight	Cost
Pomace Olive Oil	35 lbs.	$90.00
Coconut Oil	50 lbs.	$65.00
Palm Oil	50 lbs.	$105.00
Rice Bran Oil	35 lbs.	$125.00
Shipping		$60.00

(We will use the previous NaOH purchase order)

PO from "Essential Lye Station Co."

Item	Weight	Cost
NaOH	128 lbs.	$180.00
Shipping		$100.00

Now the new recipe:

Ingredients	Quantity
Pomace Olive Oil	12 oz.
Coconut Oil	24 oz.
Palm Oil	12 oz.
Rice Bran Oil	12 oz.
NaOH	8.88 oz.
Yield:	20 Bars

Running the same calculation formula as before, and adding the same amount of labor, our costs come out looking like this:

Cost of Production, 20 Bars

Item	Amount
Materials Cost	$11.25
Labor Cost	$25.00
Total Manufacturing Cost	**$36.21**

$36.21/20 bars = $1.81 per bar

After changing the recipe and keeping the labor the same, the cost of the bar drops 14 cents, from $1.95 to $1.81. Let's keep in mind that the packaging costs for both examples are the same, 16 cents. For packaging, increasing our economy of scale and buying in larger quantities is the key solution to lowering costs. Serious handcrafted soap wholesalers should look at packaging in the range of 10 cents or less per bar.

Therefore, if we reduce our packaging costs to 10 cents in our example, the bar cost comes down to $1.75. **This is of course without receiving volume discounts, as the inexpensive bar recipe example is**

from oils still purchased by the pail. Depending on the vendors you use, buying in large volumes can reduce the overall cost of a bar of soap by as much as 15 percent or more (Most raw material providers require you to call for a price on bulk quantities). If a 15 percent drop in material cost stands in our example, the cost of our wholesale bar dwindles to $1.49. After rounding up a penny, you can very easily markup 100 percent to reach a very reasonable wholesale price ($3.00 per bar), all the while still allocating $25 per hour in labor. **Furthermore, if you wanted to charge $3.50 to $4.00 wholesale for this bar you certainly could, generating a much higher margin per bar.**

Remember, purchasing managers are going to want you to tell them what price they should sell your bar of soap. This is the suggested retail price, or SRP. Traditionally, retailers always strive for the "keystone" markup, which is simply double the amount you charge them per bar (100 percent). Retailers will want to charge as much as possible initially so that there is wiggle room for putting items on sale and still making a profit. In the inexpensive bar of soap example above, a retailer might charge $5.99 initially (they would keystone your $3.00 bar), but if the soap is not moving fast enough for their liking, they can then put it on sale for $5.49 and still make a decent profit per bar. Keep this in mind when approaching purchasing managers and make sure everything you say is mirrored in all of your printed selling materials.

Finally, keep in mind that this example is still just utilizing a batch that yields 20 bars. Scaling up your production through bigger and better equipment will create much more efficiency and far less labor per bar. The key to successfully wholesaling is to continue to push yourself and your business to cut costs while still creating a quality product.

Your Products, Your Pricing

Pricing your soap should be a very well thought out, thoroughly researched project. You can take bits and pieces of this chapter and create a plan to get your costs down as much as possible. **I will re-emphasize here that if you believe a certain price you set, no matter what it is, will be successful, than by all means set that price**! Again, in my experience in dealings with my wholesale customers, the higher the price I set, the less sales I ultimately made in their stores. Finding that sweet spot is crucial to longevity in the marketplace. I sincerely hope you find yours.

Chapter Summary

— Every penny counts when it comes to wholesaling.

— **Value perception** can be defined as the worth that a product has in the mind of the consumer. The consumer's perceived value of a product affects the price that he or she is willing to pay.

— If you don't currently have SoapMaker Professional™ or another software program that tracks your material costs, purchases, postage, and labor such as Craftybase™ (www.craftybase.com), now would be a good time to obtain one.

  — **Nonetheless, follow the guided steps in this chapter to find your truest cost, down to the unit of measure you use to make a batch of soap.**

— **Adding Labor Costs**: You need to come up with your own methodology and do it quickly!

  — *How much do you want to be paid per hour of work?*

— A **markup** is defined as the amount added to your cost price to arrive at a selling price and is a commonly used technique in determining how much to charge for your products.

— Profit – Total Manufacturing Cost = Profit Margin

— Profit Margin / Profit = Profit Margin Percentage

— Purchasing managers are going to want you to tell them at what price they should sell your bar of soap. This is the suggested retail price, or SRP.

— Are your soaps and bodycare products valued commodities that will warrant repeat purchases, or are they a special, niche gift? **Your price ultimately determines this.**

— Two Easy Ways to Lower Costs:

  — Economy of Scale

  — Change Your Recipe

Scaling up your production through bigger and better equipment will create much more efficiency and far less labor per bar.

Chapter 7

Paperwork

My brother (and business partner) Christopher always says, "Conducting business is really just filling out the paperwork." After being in business for this long, I'd say he's absolutely right. Getting all of your paperwork and any marketing materials in order and having it readily available will turn sales potentials into customers. **Purchasing managers are going to expect some professional marketing materials from you, primarily a wholesale catalog**. If the stars align and they want to make an opening order, they will then expect some standard paperwork, such as your W-9 and certificate of insurance.

Wholesale Catalog

If you are serious about wholesaling, you will need a catalog. A wholesale catalog shows the purchasing manager that you have your prices and products in order and that you are ready to do business in an efficient and timely manner. The content of the catalog should be tastefully designed, but also precise and to the point. At the end of the day, purchasing managers want to know how much they have to purchase to cover the minimum order and how much it is going to cost. I've had fancy wholesale catalogs printed in the past, but I discovered that the extra expense wasn't really worth it. While I always hire professional help in the design, I stick with 8.5 x 11 standard U.S. Paper dimensions and print from my office as needed.

Wholesale Catalog Components

Page 1) Cover Page
Contents:
—— High-resolution picture of your product or products
—— Company name / logo
—— Company tagline

— Contact information:
  — Name of the wholesale manager of your company
  — Company phone number
  — Ordering email address
  — Website

Page 2) Company Profile Page
Contents:

This page could offer the reader your mission statement and some values of the business. A nice profile picture of the business owner can be added here if you like. On this page, I like to let potential retailers know where the manufacturing, fulfillment and business operations are done.

Page 3) Products and Pricing Page
Contents:

This is your main content page. Display your product pictures attractively and evenly on the page. Provide a brief description of each product and the varieties therein. This page should also include your wholesale price along with the SRP (suggested retail price).

Page 4) Retailer Obligations Page

Contents:

This page provides retailers with everything they need to know for their ongoing relationship with you.

— Minimum order (See Chapter, "Logistics")
— Opening order discount
    — If any, I recommend up to 15 percent off before shipping.
— Shipping terms (See Chapter, "Logistics")
— Payment terms
    — The standard is Net 30, which means that the retail customer has 30 days to pay you after receiving the order.
— Any return policies you might have, for example:
    — *If you receive damaged product, please contact us within five business days.*
    — *We will replace or provide credit for products that are damaged during shipment if they are returned to us; however, we cannot refund or credit shipping costs.*

Page 5) Outreach Page
Contents:

If your business is not currently helping someone in someway, then start! A business outreach program will not only help you sleep better, but you can also showcase your philanthropic efforts on a page in your wholesale catalog. This shows your potential buyer that you are thinking beyond just revenue.

A Quick Word on Business Outreach...

Cause marketing refers to a type of marketing involving the cooperative efforts of a for-profit business and a non-profit organization for mutual benefit.

If you are looking to partner with a great non-profit organization that tackles some powerful world issues like hygiene and women's empowerment through economic development, check out

www.lovinsoaproject.org to see how you can get involved!

Benjamin D. Aaron

[Cover Page Example]

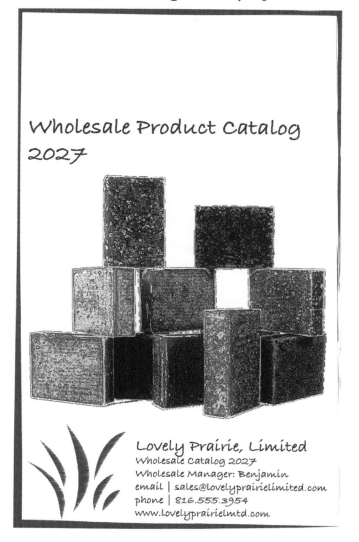

Wholesale Product Catalog 2027

Lovely Prairie, Limited
Wholesale Catalog 2027
Wholesale Manager: Benjamin
email | sales@lovelyprairielimited.com
phone | 816.555.3954
www.lovelyprairielmtd.com

[Company Profile Page Example]

Our mission is to live in the presence of nature, and to inspire our local and global communities into a shared sense of belonging and respect for the same, by hand-crafting an elevated everyday product and recurrently engaging in social and environmental endeavors.

Business Operations: Kansas City, MO
Manufacuturing Operations: Austin, TX

Lovely Prairie, Limited
Wholesale Catalog 2027
Wholesale Manager: Benjamin
email | sales@lovelyprairielimited.com
phone | 816.555.3954
www.lovelyprairielmtd.com

[Products & Pricing Page Example]

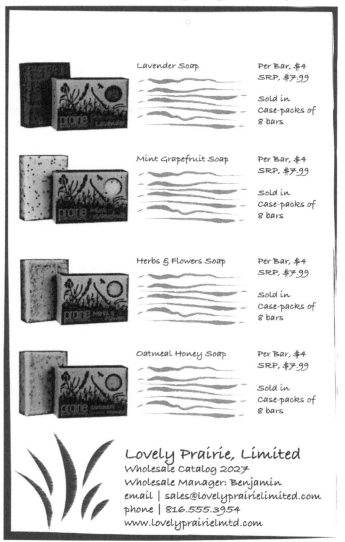

Lavender Soap

Per Bar, $4
SRP, $7.99

Sold in
Case-packs of
8 bars

Mint Grapefruit Soap

Per Bar, $4
SRP, $7.99

Sold in
Case-packs of
8 bars

Herbs & Flowers Soap

Per Bar, $4
SRP, $7.99

Sold in
Case-packs of
8 bars

Oatmeal Honey Soap

Per Bar, $4
SRP, $7.99

Sold in
Case-packs of
8 bars

Lovely Prairie, Limited
Wholesale Catalog 2027
Wholesale Manager: Benjamin
email | sales@lovelyprairielimited.com
phone | 816.555.3954
www.lovelyprairielmtd.com

[Retailer Obligations Page Example]

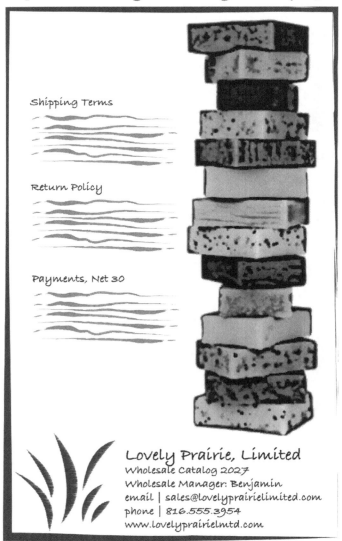

Shipping Terms

Return Policy

Payments, Net 30

Lovely Prairie, Limited
Wholesale Catalog 2027
Wholesale Manager: Benjamin
email | sales@lovelyprairielimited.com
phone | 816.555.3954
www.lovelyprairielmtd.com

[Outreach Page Example]

In Conjunction with
The Lovin' Soap Project, Lovely Prairie...

Lovely Prairie, Limited
Wholesale Catalog 2027
Wholesale Manager: Benjamin
email | sales@lovelyprairielimited.com
phone | 816.555.3954
www.lovelyprairielmtd.com

At The Very Least,

Display Your Products and Pricing

I've seen decorative wholesale catalogs from folks in our industry, some of which have been printed in bulk. This is of course okay to do, but keep in mind that prices, ingredients or even shipping terms can change, so it is good to be prepared to change any information on your catalog if needed. This is why I stick to a very nicely designed catalog, but one I can print myself. Again, the most important thing is that you get your pricing, products and any pertinent ordering information in a clear, readable format for your potential customer.

Keep In Mind File Size...
Many large retail chains have a kilobyte limit to what their employees can send and receive through email. Because of this, I have a print version and an email version. My email version is just under 3,000 KB.

Form W-9

Form W-9 – Request for Taxpayer Identification Number and Certification – is one of the most commonly used IRS forms. Both individuals and entities use the W-9 form to provide their taxpayer identification number to entities that will pay them during the tax year. Once your potential customer has agreed to an opening order, they may request that you provide a W-9 so they can accurately report the payments they make to you over the course of the current tax year.

Completing Form W-9

To complete Form W-9, you'll need to enter your full name as shown on your federal income tax return on the first line. If you are operating a business under a separate name, you should enter that on the second line. Most employed and self-employed taxpayers will select "Individual/Sole Proprietor." Professionals who operate partnerships, corporations or estates should select the appropriate classification for their situation. If you're running your own business and you have an employer identification number, you should enter that number next to the EIN field.

The easiest thing to do is to fill out a W-9 and scan it into your computer. Keep this file in a folder entitled, "Wholesale Paperwork." As soon as you land a new wholesale account, you will have it ready to send to them. Most everyone accepts W-9s via email or fax.

Certificate of Insurance

Most retail outlets require that you have product liability insurance. As it relates to wholesaling soap, product liability insurance protects the retail business from claims related to the manufacture or sale of the products they carry and sell to the public. It covers the seller's liability for losses or injuries to a buyer by a defect or malfunction of the product, and, in some instances, a defective design or a failure to warn. If needed, your policy would pay for any damage or injury (within the limits of the coverage provided) resulting from the use of the insured's goods.

Insurance Policies and Coverage

There are industry specific insurance policies for the handcrafted soapmaker. Though your options are seemingly endless when it comes to insurance coverage and policies, here are four that have the handcrafter's situation in mind.

— **Handmade Artisan Insurance**

https://www.handmadeinsurance.com

— **Indie Business Network**

http://www.indiebusinessnetwork.com

— **Handcrafted Soap and Cosmetic Guild**

http://soapguild.org

— **RLI Home Business Insurance**

https://www.insuremyhomebiz.com/

Most product liability insurance offers $1 million in coverage. You can increase your coverage to $2 million for an additional annual fee, usually around $50 - $60 extra. **For most large retail outlets, $2 million in coverage is required, so keep this in mind as you shop for insurance.**

Resale Certificate

Finally, there is one thing you need from all of your retailers. Though this certificate is comprised and issued on the state-level, thus varying greatly, you as the wholesaler should request a **resale certificate** from all retailers you do business with. The purpose of a resale certificate is to allow a business to buy goods without paying local sales tax on them. Thus, it is that business's responsibility to collect the tax from the customer when they sell an item. Your business, the wholesaler, is to request to see the resale certificate as proof that the goods are being purchased for resale. A resale certificate will typically state the name and address of the buyer, the reseller's permit number, a description of the goods being purchased, and a statement that the goods are being purchased for resale.

Retailers are accustomed to providing the resale certificate to all of their vendors, so don't hesitate to ask for it. This is just a safety mechanism in the chain of moving products and information from business to business. If and when your business gets audited, they will ask if you have obtained resale certificates from all of your retail customers. If you cannot provide them, they may assume you have sold products without collecting and remitting sales tax.

Chapter Summary

— If you are serious about wholesaling, you will need a catalog. A wholesale catalog shows the purchasing manager that you have your prices and products in order and that you are ready to do business in an efficient and timely manner.

— Wholesale Materials Folder (on your computer):
  — Wholesale Catalog, Print Version
  — Wholesale Catalog, Email Version
  — Scanned Copy of Form W-9
  — Copy of Certificate of Insurance With Product Liability Coverage of $2 Million.

During the sell-phase, you will have delivered the catalog. After the sale, simply send your new wholesale client the rest of these materials and ask for their resale certificate. Though it sounds like a lot, having everything handy makes the process much easier. And, every major retailer will ask for these documents, so you might as well get used to it. It should be just as much a part of your business as mixing lye.

Create a new folder somewhere on your laptop or computer and name it, "Wholesale Materials." After obtaining everything covered in the list above, drop all of them in the folder, give yourself a pat on the back and go have a beer or green tea.

Chapter 8

Logistics

Knowing exactly what and how much you are going to sell to each and every potential customer will qualm your manufacturing fears and allow you to assert a firm production schedule so you can meet the demand of incoming orders. Let's talk about what it is you are selling, and how to hone that into commodity-driven products that are easy to make, pack, ship and/or personally deliver. Moreover, let's discuss how to make things not only easier on you (the manufacturer and seller and oftentimes dishwasher and everything else), but also your customers.

Product Line

How many different soaps should you wholesale?

Many soapmakers are offering a wide variety of soaps on their websites and other selling platforms. If you just look around online at our peers, you can see what other soapmakers are offering via retail, or directly from the source (the manufacturer and proprietor). *So how do you know how big an offering you can make to wholesale customers?*

I realized rather quickly that I was too big for my britches in the world of wholesale when I sold 18 different varieties of soap to multiple retail outlets. At the time, I was usually the only one making soap, and I was the only one selling. This meant a lot of phoning, emailing, invoicing, ordering and driving around town, on top of all the production responsibilities. This went on for years. It was too much for me, and it was beginning to show in my work, not to mention my life outside of work. All the while, my company was working on opening up a retail store that would be open every day of the week in a community-centered retail-shopping outlet. I knew I had to make a change, so I did.

We reduced our offerings from 18 to 8. Almost immediately my stress levels plummeted. **And surprise-**

surprise, our revenue went up. The end consumers in all of our retail outlets were generally only buying the most popular of the 18 bars, leaving the less popular ones to collect dust. Having only our top sellers on the shelves created more purchases from the end consumer, which ultimately meant more orders from each store's purchasing manager.

Your situation is ultimately yours. It is your responsibility to find your perfect array of soaps to offer retail outlets. **Depending on how, where and how often you produce soap, make a realistic projection of the total number of varieties you feel comfortable making in large quantities and go from there. Some of my favorite (and very successful) soap companies offer only two to six different varieties via wholesale.**

Lastly, keep in mind the soap-design factor. As stated in the introduction of this book, I am a "plain bars" soapmaker when it comes to design. I do not make elaborately detailed, beautifully swirled soaps and the like. I don't have the patience, and it just isn't my personal style! The reason I bring this up is to say that if you are planning on wholesaling a very intricately designed soap, make sure you can scale up appropriately and replicate that same intricate design every single time you produce it, whether you make a 20-bar batch or a 200-bar batch. **Customers need to see consistency, so keep in mind what you are capable of, in labor, quantity, variety, design and packaging.**

Minimum Order

The minimum order you mandate to purchasing managers should not only be worth your while, but directly tied to how you ship. At Prairie Soap Company, we have what we call "case packs," which are rectangular boxes that snuggly hold eight bars of fully packaged soap. This is how we wholesale any particular variety of soap. We obtain our case pack boxes in bulk from Uline™ (www.uline.com).

Thus, if a purchasing manager from a retail store wants Lavender soap, she would have to order in multiples of eight units (eight soaps), as that is how we shipp out in the case packs. Never will I allow a retail outlet order less than eight units of any variety. This makes things simple for both parties. If Lavender soap is ordered, eight packaged bars will be placed in a case pack. Our initial (opening) order offers **one case pack per variety**, which comprises eight different varieties. Thus, the minimum amount of soap any store can originally purchase is 64. This is a comfortable number for my business, as it allows us to sell to hundreds of stores at a capacity that we are comfortable with and know we can produce. **Finding your magic number of minimum units to sell will ultimately be up to you, but if you are just starting out, keep it simple and within your grasp.**

Our minimum reorder is four case packs, or 32 total bars of soap (4 soaps x 8 = 32 total bars). Anything less than this is not considered a great use of time or shipping. Though I certainly prefer to sell 64 soaps on every single order, most large chain retail outlets ask that we honor a reorder minimum, rather than forcing them to purchase a full order of 64 units, or eight case packs. This allows them to keep as low an inventory as possible at all times, which is key for running an efficient retail outlet. **Thus, on all opening orders, the bare minimum a store can order is 64 soaps, or eight case packs of eight different varieties. The bare minimum that same store can reorder is 32 soaps, or four case packs.**

Because of this order structure, we obtained what we call the "master box" and the "reorder box" from

Uline (www.uline.com). The **master box** snuggly fits eight case packs for initial orders (or any orders that large for that matter), and the **reorder box** snuggly fits four case packs, which is the reorder minimum. We realized that most retail outlets would order the minimum amount when they could, as previously stated. For this reason, we designed the following system for orders and shipment:

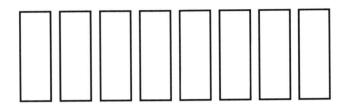

8 Soaps fit snuggly into a "case-pack".

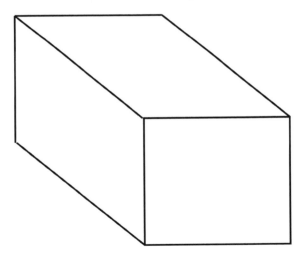

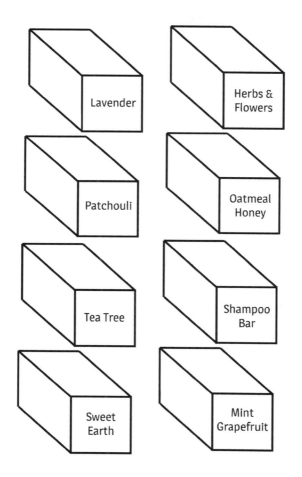

8 case-pack boxes of 8 different soaps go into the masterbox.

Master Box, Side View (cross-section)

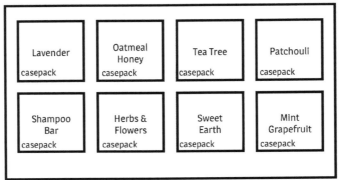

Master Box, Top View

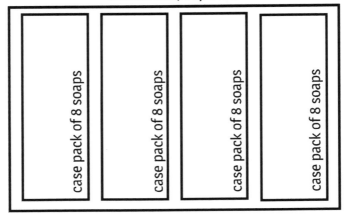

Reorder Box, Side View (cross-section)

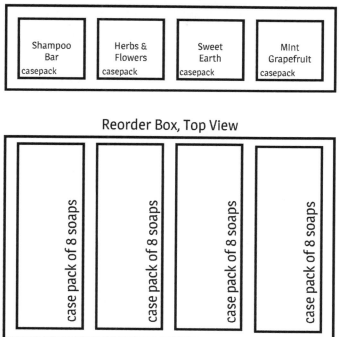

Reorder Box, Top View

This system works great for us. It was somewhat serendipitous to find the correctly sized master box, reorder box and case pack boxes from a major supplier such as Uline™. This may or may not be the case for your business. Using the boxes limited my usage of bubble wrap and the dreaded shipping peanuts, as everything was more than secure just using boxes shipped in boxes. It is streamlined and sturdy for shipment, and cuts down on the labor involved in packing peanuts, bubble wrap, etc.

The upfront cost of operating your wholesale logistics this way is higher than just putting your soap in a box filled with bubble wrap, peanuts, etc., but I cannot stress enough the time factor. **Your time as the business owner should be utilized in the absolute best way possible**. If you are constantly fumbling around for shipping materials, grabbing boxes from wherever you can find them and cramming the last bar in the box sideways, upside down and backwards just to make it fit, you are probably using too much of your valuable time, and you aren't leaving a great impression with your wholesale customer by having a cluttered shipment of product.

Also keep in mind that more and more buyers are requesting that vendors not use Styrofoam™ peanuts, due to their environmental impact. Whole Foods Market™ (among many others), for example, does not allow vendors to utilize Styrofoam™ peanuts in their shipments.

This is our method – this is not the only way to do things. Some soapmaking companies would consider my ordering schematic too small, others too big. Wholesaling takes a lot of forethought, so make sure to really think this process through. Be as cost effective as you possibly can, and at the same time, as efficient as possible. Set up a system from front to back that is easy to manage and above all else, make your soaps and other offerings practical to produce at a high level.

Shipping

Shipping will absolutely make or break your business in multiple ways. If you don't plan out your shipping strategy, you could end up unprofitable, as you are already selling your soap at half the price.

Something to Consider…

Because the retail outlet opportunities for cottage soap and bodycare products have exploded in the last decade, more and more purchasing managers want shipping, packaging and presentation to be part of an overall pleasing purchasing experience. How can you improve their purchasing experience?

Cost Strategy: Shipping

Shipping can often be a mystery. Little costs can really add up quickly. Every time you ship, examine what you just shipped with great clarity. Step back and look at every input of an order:

— Total Cost of Order in Materials
— Total Cost of Order in Packaging
— Total Cost of Order in Labor
— Total Shipping Cost (include shipping materials)
— Credit Card Fee (if applicable)

Charging Shipping On an Order

Yes, you charge your wholesale customers shipping. And knowing the right amount to charge customers for shipping is profoundly important to business success. You don't want to charge too little because that would hurt your profits, but you also don't want to charge too much because that would make you less competitive. **It may be best to simply focus on breaking even.**

Shipping Factors To Consider:

There are a number of ways that you can charge for shipping to ensure you don't lose money, and at the same time, better market your total offer to your customers. Let's discuss some of the factors to consider in determining how much to charge for shipping and handling.

Calculated Or Flat Rate Shipping?

Generally speaking, there are two main options you have for how to price your shipped products: 1) **calculated shipping** and 2) **flat-rate shipping**. Let's discuss the advantages of each:

Calculated Shipping

To figure out your shipping costs you need to actually calculate them. Before you start selling your soap to retail outlets, measure their weight, dimensions, and other factors that affect how much it costs to ship them. Round these numbers up to the nearest whole number. On the websites of all major couriers is a place to calculate the cost based on all of the parameters stated above. **If you know the specific retail store you are targeting, you could go as far as modifying your wholesale catalog per customer to showcase what the shipping cost**

will be for that particular store. This is a little extra upfront work, but will create zero confusion for that retailer on what your terms are in the selling process. This is what my company does.

Flat-Rate Shipping

Flat-rate shipping involves averaging out all of the costs of your company's shipments. You might lose money on half of your shipments and you might make money on the other half, so it could all even out in the end. In using the flat-rate method, pay close attention to your average cost of shipment, as it will change over time. This will be what you charge all customers, which is why it is so important to keep track of the average cost. If you let overall costs rise without adjusting your average, you'll start losing money. You also want to allow the flat rate to fall if your average cost falls, as well. **The key is to be responsive**. Flat-rate shipping is a good idea for many businesses that want to keep things simple for their customers. It works best for products that are fairly small and not too heavy, which can be seen as a disadvantage with soap, as it is fairly heavy.

No matter how you decide to ship, your shipping price strategy is part of your overall effort to be profitable. You should treat it like any other part of your business. Shipping can be a source of profit as long as you don't go overboard and drive customers away by charging too much. Though it of course isn't technically producing a profit, breaking even on shipping costs over a calendar year is seen as a success in my company.

Courier Business Accounts

Once you have decided on the carriers you want to use, consider setting up business accounts. Business accounts offer a variety of services including discounts, better expense tracking and a whole host of online tools to more efficiently manage the shipping aspects of your business.

— USPS Business Gateway
— Canada Post Venture One
— UK Royal Mail Online
— Australia Post Business Credit Account
— UPS Business Solutions
— FedEx Business Center

Figuring Out Your Own Schematic

Shipping is definitely a challenging aspect to any wholesale business. Your business will have its own unique challenges to work through and overcome to develop the best and most efficient shipping strategy. Like many aspects of building a new business, it will take time and tweaking to determine what works best.

Understanding all the variables and evolving your shipping strategy with your growing business is vital to its long-term health and success. So once you think you have it figured out, don't let it go stale. Reevaluate every quarter to make sure you're delivering the absolute best possible service and experience for the best possible price to your customers.

And remember that you can always change things. The first step in logistics is figuring out what and how you are going to sell to as many retail outlets as you can. The next step is to determine the shipping. If you are going to start out local, as many do, that is great, but there should still be a shipping and time/labor factor in personal deliveries (for example, I charge a 'Direct Service Delivery' fee of $5 for myself or company representative who personally drops off a local order). **Everything costs money in business, so make sure you really**

think through your minimum order and shipping charges.

Chapter Summary

— Depending on how, where and how often you produce soap, make a realistic projection of the total number of varieties you feel comfortable making in large quantities for wholesaling.

— Finding your magic number of minimum units to sell will ultimately be up to you, but if you are just starting out, keep it simple and within your grasp.

— If you are planning on wholesaling a very intricately designed soap, make sure you can scale up appropriately and replicate that same intricate design every single time you produce it, whether you make a 20-bar batch or a 200-bar batch.

— Examine The Entire Cost Of Every Order:
    — Total Cost of Order in Materials
    — Total Cost of Order in Packaging
    — Total Cost of Order in Labor
    — Total Shipping Cost (include shipping materials)
    — Credit Card Fee (if applicable)

— Generally speaking, there are two main options you have for how to price your shipped products:

  — Calculated shipping

  — Flat-rate shipping

— Do you actually know that you can produce a certain amount of your product within a specific timeframe?

  — Retailers will want to know the turnaround time when they place an order.

— Everything costs money in business, so make sure you really think through your minimum order and shipping charges.

— **If possible, research and make a sophisticated projection of what shipping an order will cost to each individual wholesale customer you have, and then modify your wholesale catalog for that particular customer so there is zero confusion.**

Chapter 9

Selling

Finding new retail customers to buy your products is obviously an important part of the entire sales process. You may have a really great product line, but aren't finding the right buyers. I've seen firsthand from fellow soapmakers the major reason why this occurs. It is the propensity to procrastinate on doing the scary things, like cold calling or walking into stores to introduce their business and offer samples, etc. There are easy steps you can take to qualm your selling fears and create long-lasting relationships, even if you initially receive the runaround or negative feedback. And always remember, you are helping a purchasing manager do their job by providing a quality product. This should always be your mindset while selling.

That Being Said, I Preface the Chapter With This:

If you have all of your materials and paperwork ready, especially your wholesale catalog along with your shipping terms for the specific customer you have targeted, you are 95 percent there. Storeowners, retail outlet purchasing managers and especially regional buyers (for large chain retailers) just simply don't have a lot of time to talk to you, and believe me; they will let you know that! Thus, if you can show them you have everything ready to go, all they have to do is say, "Yes."

Know The Benefits Of Your Products

Before you go marching into your targeted retail outlet, let's write down a synopsis of your products and the benefit of using them. **People don't buy products; they buy the results that the products will provide them**. Make a list of all of the benefits that your customer will enjoy by using your soap and bodycare products. This will almost immediately calm your nerves when it comes to selling. You now won't be selling four ounces of saponified fatty acids; you will be selling the *benefits* that those four ounces provide.

On a clean sheet of paper, write down all of the benefits that your soap and bodycare products will provide. In a free writing style, write down anything and everything that comes to mind about the different and unique qualities your products have. Do you use essential oils to scent your soap? Write down the aroma-therapeutic benefits of each essential oil of each soap variety. Do you incorporate any additives into your recipes, such as oats, lavender buds or comfrey leaf powder? Research and write out all of the benefits that these additives provide for the skin. You aren't making any health claims here – you are simply building a solid foundation for the selling process. Do your bars last a long time? Do they have a rich, consistent lather due to all of the wonderful castor oil you use?

Whatever you can think of, write it down. Always remember that you know more than the person you are selling to, so don't take for granted what ingredients are in your products. The fact is, most people hear certain terms and concepts in our industry and engage some interest, but they don't know the *reasons* behind why certain ingredients are so good for us. This is your chance to really explain, not about your soap, but the *benefits* of your soap, due to the foresight and care you have taken to add the appropriate ingredients to make wholesome, well-worth-it products that customers will buy.

What Problem Are You Solving?

If you have identified your customers correctly, they will pay you to solve their problems. What kind of problem does your customer have that you can solve? Sometimes the problems are obvious and clear, like people who have skin irritations, etc. Sometimes the problems are not obvious, such as chronic dry skin; so they don't know there is actually soap out there that will dramatically improve dry skin (which would be yours).

Whatever the case may be, look around for the problem and if you are creative and clever, you will find the solution. For example, you are in a retail store that you would like to have a business partnership with, and you notice that all of the current bars of soap do not have avocado oil in them. You can then present to the purchasing manager all of the great benefits that avocado oil provides the skin and explain that your soaps contain an abundance of the nourishing oil. In this case, we are using a very direct form of market research to make a sale and solving a problem at the same time.

Your Competitive Advantage

Your competitive advantage is the reason for buying your products, in terms of the benefits, results and outcomes that your customer will enjoy; results that they will *not* receive from using the products of your competitors. Focus on the benefits of what makes your product better than others. This is directly tied to problem solving as well.

After you have exhausted your list of benefits, refine them into a strong sales pitch. **Make sure you do your homework on the other soap and bodycare products in the retail outlet you are targeting. However, never call out the negatives of another soap company; this is bad form**. I don't even bring up the topic. Nonetheless, I have been in multiple selling situations where the purchasing manager asks me why *my* soap is better than the soaps she currently sells. This is where creating your competitive advantage on paper comes in. Instead of directly pointing out a disadvantage of a competitor's product, teach your potential business partner the benefits of your soap.

Your Sales Pitch

I have tried every method I could think of to sell my soap to retail outlets. I have cold-called, emailed, walked in to stores, and even turned in a bunch of those "How Can We Do Better" slips, letting the store know that "I" would love to see soap from a business called "Prairie Soap Company" in the store!

With an array of options from which to choose, I believe, from personal experience that the best way to get a serious wholesale client relationship going is by calling the store and asking for the soap and bodycare manager, or just walking right in (if local). When I relate to fellow soapmakers how my company gets into so many stores, they will often shutter with anxiety or nervously laugh it off, as if to say, "Well, this just isn't for me. I'm not a salesperson."

So maybe you're not a salesperson. Neither am I. I never sold a thing in my life before I started my soap business. But sales mean revenue. Revenue means money in your pocket. Money in your pocket means you can do the things you were put on Earth to do. **This is the place in life where you have to really assess what you and your business are all about. If you want to wholesale your products, you will have to get on the phone**. For me, my livelihood depends on it. I put all of my chips into my business, so I don't have the luxury of being laissez faire about selling. If I am going to eat and pay my bills, I am going to get on that phone and call. If your lot in life were such that you don't *have* to make a sale if you don't want to, I would reconsider your reasons for wanting to wholesale in the first place, and what owning a business really means to you.

You can cold call in person or by phone. If you are local to a store you would like to be in, pick between what is going to be most comfortable for both parties and just go for it. If you are not local, don't be afraid to pick up the phone and start calling.

Cold Calling Tips

Cold calling potential prospects can be scary and often frustrating. Whether you are doing it in person or on the phone, it is your job to warm up a potential customer.

This can be exceedingly difficult, especially if you're new to the process. Here are a few tricks to make it easier.

Give Them All of the Attention and Focus.

In your initial contact with a purchasing manager, focus every part of your attention and your questions on him or her. Don't talk at great length about yourself and what you do. I don't even talk about my company all that much during my initial contact. I simply let all of the focus be on them.

Client-centered selling is, ironically professional, as the focus is on his or her needs as a fellow professional; but having the focus on them and being genuine opens up a certain lightheartedness that is almost like a quick-forming *personal* relationship. It took me a while to figure out this technique, but as soon as I allowed all of my questions to be both genuine and 100 percent about them, their business, their position within the business, and their needs, selling then became incredibly easy.

— *How long have you been with the company?*

— *How long have you owned your own business?*

— *When did you start carrying handmade soaps?*

— *What do you enjoy most about your job?*

Plan Your Questions In Advance.

In cold calling, the more information you can elicit, the easier it will be for you to qualify the prospect and then go on to make a sale. This is where questioning is so important. Your questions should be thought out carefully in advance, and organized in a logical sequence, from the most general to the most specific.

Less Is More.

When you approach a prospect in person for the first time, one strategy is for you to "go in naked." What this means is that, at the most, you carry a simple folder rather than a briefcase full of brochures or soap samples. If the prospect is interested and wants a presentation and more information, you can always go back to your car to get what you need. But when you go in without all of that stuff, you lower the stress of initial sales resistance and cause the prospect to relax and open up to you sooner. Although prospecting in person is often the scariest, it is very effective if you are not too pushy or take up too much of their time.

In my experience, cold calling in person requires you to really read the room, so to speak. Most purchasing managers are always busy, and they have a lot on their minds, due to all of the product stock they are in charge of. If it isn't a good time for them, just try again later. If you catch them at a good time, take advantage of it by being well prepared. **And of course, offer the biggest, most engaging smile you can possibly produce.**

Don't Attempt To Sell On Your First Cold Call.

In your first call, you should never attempt to sell your soap and bodycare products. Instead, your focus should be on information gathering. It should almost feel like a really comfortable interview, where you are asking all of the questions to the prospect. Take notes and tell them you will come back. Focus on building the relationship and coming across as friendly, genial and nonthreatening.

The longer your prospect remains relaxed, and the more he or she opens up to you, the more likely you will make the sale. If you are cold calling on the phone, make sure to smile throughout the entire conversation and try to stay in one place instead of pacing. Relax. Your energy will be picked up and shared by your prospect.

Find Out Exactly What Benefit Will Cause Your Customer To Buy From You.

With each potential customer, there is a key benefit that will trigger buying desire and cause the customer to purchase your soap and bodycare products. At the same time, there is usually a key **fear** or doubt that will hold the customer back from buying. Your initial job, in your first cold call, is to find out exactly what benefit will cause this customer to buy from you, and exactly what fear or doubt might hold this customer back. In my experience, all fears from prospects generally involve price, branding, and whether or not I can keep up with the orders as they come in.

Don't Be Afraid To Ask For More.

Don't be afraid to ask. "Ask" is the magic word for sales success. You can even say,

"Mr. Prospect, we have found that there is always a key benefit or major reason that a person would purchase our soaps. What might it be for you?"

If you are open, honest, and genuine, and ask out of curiosity, you will be amazed at the answers you'll hear. Prospects will often give you all the information that you need to make a sale. The key for you is to ask.

186

The Follow-Up

The follow up is much easier than the cold call, as you already know each other and the tone has been set. I never let too much time pass before a phone call or in-person meeting – 10 days or less. This is more than enough time for them to mull it over and try out your nice sample bar of soap. And by this time, maybe one of their family members has tried it, bringing up a conversation in their home about your soap. This can lend itself to good vibes about you and your product in the eyes of the purchasing manager. **You just never know**. Once I thought I lost a sale only to nervously call to follow-up and find that the purchasing manager's entire family had a long conversation over dinner about the sample soap in the bathroom, what was in it, and why it felt so good, etc. He loved it and took an order right away.

On another occasion, after pitching my soaps to a potential client, the purchasing manager simply said "No" and said nothing else. She was downright cold and extremely distant. I said "Okay, no worries. Thank you very much for your time. Have a good day." I turned around and walked away with my full bar sample still in my hand. I then walked back and handed her the bar of soap. I told her that I brought it in, so I might as well leave it with someone. She didn't even look me in the eye, but did squeak out a murmured "Thank you." I knew I obviously wasn't getting this sale and moved on with my day. But to my surprise, she called me the next day absolutely raving about the soap I gave her. She told me that her husband's dry, cracked knuckles felt better and almost immediately looked better after trying it. She was hooked after she defiantly told me no. **You just never know**. Soap is such a personal thing in life. Take advantage of this.

If you are afraid to cold call, it is okay; you should be, as it is a nerve-wracking thing to do. But I suggest that you simply feel the fear and do it anyway. The worst thing anyone can ever say to you is "no," and that is okay. **Always remember, if they say "no," you say "next".**

Calm Your Nerves.

You're Already A Salesperson!

From the time you get up in the morning until the time you go to bed at night, you are constantly negotiating, communicating, persuading, influencing and trying to get people to cooperate with you and do the things that you want them to do. This is, at the very least, an indirect form of sales.

In this daily-life example, if you are poor at these types of interactive sales, then you are merely a recipient of influence. This means that you will be continually influenced and persuaded by others. If you are good at these types of indirect sales, it means that you will be an agent of influence and you will be constantly influencing and persuading others in the direction you want them to go. If you look at *business* sales in this way, you can see that sales and leadership are not too distant cousins.

All effective parents are wonderful salespeople. All effective children are very good at selling ideas to their parents. Excellent employees are very effective at getting their bosses to do things and getting their coworkers to cooperate with them in getting the job done. Anyone who is effective in virtually any area of life that involves other people is an excellent salesperson of some kind.

In order for your wholesale business to run smoothly and efficiently, you are to become very, very good at selling. There is, no doubt, a stigma to selling. I have mentioned often at speaking engagements my initial mindset towards selling and how I had a naïve consensus about what it really meant to sell. People associate selling with being a low-level activity that can feel pushy and uncomfortable. You can't get a degree in selling. There isn't a Department of Selling at your local university. This is ironic, as about 15 million Americans make their living selling. It is still the largest, single, identifiable occupational group in the United States. Sales are what move and shake industries. **Salespeople are key in creating a demand for just about anything our society consumes.**

If you have a mindset about selling that feels shady and awkward, I can guarantee it will come out in your sales pitch. Just be you, and realize that all purchasing managers you will speak to are accustomed to corresponding with sales people, usually on a daily basis. Just remember to ask a lot of genuine questions and be yourself.

Sending Samples And a Letter:

A Quick Story

I wasn't exactly sure how to approach all of the national chain retailers that we eventually sold products to. I knew through some research that the store level doesn't really have purchasing authority; it must come from the regional office. For example, the regional offices that oversee all the stores located in my area (Kansas City, MO) for both Natural Grocers™ and Whole Foods Market™ are both located in Colorado. How was I supposed to obtain a selling relationship with people from Colorado?

As briefly mentioned in Chapter 3 (in regards to my outdated soap packaging), I waltzed right into one of my local Whole Foods Markets and asked for the bodycare manager. Again, on that particular occasion noted in Chapter 3, it was not fruitful. Nonetheless, I decided to keep cold-calling the local stores, stopping in every once in a while with a full bar sample (of the new and improved packaging, see Chapter 3).

I finally connected with one of the managers who really liked my company's soaps, via the full bar sample I had given her. And so she gave me a name and address. She gave me the name and contact information of the regional buyer in Colorado. As soon as I got back to my office from that quick sales pitch, I began drafting a letter to the regional buyer. Below is the letter, copied and pasted, word for word (though I did change the regional buyer's name and store information). Accompanying this letter was our entire wholesale product line of soaps, full-size and fully packaged.

Dear Autumn,

This is Benjamin Aaron, Managing Partner & Chief Formulator of Prairie Soap Company. I recently had a wonderful visit with Alex from Store No. 835. Alex recommended that I start a relationship with you, as she is now an advocate of our products! We are a swiftly growing business, and we are trending upwardly in our marketplace. We as a business are ready to take the next step, and on behalf of everyone here; we are both prepared and excited about having a presence in Whole Foods Market.

Though we are a smaller company (compared to the larger vendors you have the fortune of working with), we are ready to take a big step in production and presence. All of the bigger vendors that you currently work with had to start somewhere, much like we are now. We are prepared to take the next step and create more national presence, and do so the right way. And we need your help. Whole Foods Market is our demographic. You are perfect for us. Our product, culture and price points are too alien for standard grocery markets. Whole Foods cares about what they are putting out, and your end-consumer knows this, and that falls right in line with what we are producing as a business environment.

We have made great strides in the last few years, greatly improved our recipes and have found a recurrent customer trend with these 8 soaps you will find in the catalog and parcel. We now have the manufacturing capacities to supply hundreds of stores, as our economy of scale has improved and we moved our business to a 2,000 square foot production/storefront in the Kansas City Metropolitan Area. We are ready to launch our business to the next level, and we need the assistance of our community, and our buyers.

I hope you enjoy our product. Have an incredible week, and I look forward to hearing from you.

Sincerely,

Benjamin D. Aaron

Exactly ten days later, I received a lovely email from Autumn. She was ready to put our products into five local-to-us stores, with the opportunity to expand indefinitely as our sales warranted. She immediately asked for all of the paperwork discussed in Chapter 7, which I was able to immediately attach with my reply.

This is what I mean by being genuine and honest. I told the regional buyer the absolute truth, that we were a very small business compared to many vendors she works with, but that we *would* meet production capabilities and their expectations as a brand. And so we did. If I had not been persistent in cold-calling and offering samples on the local store level, nor sent the letter with full-bar samples, I wouldn't have stood a chance to enter that retail outlet chain. I did the *exact* same thing for the following health market chains; Natural Grocers™, Lucky's™, Sprouts™, and The Fresh Market™, all of whom have regional buyers outside of my local area, and they all took orders within a few weeks of my sending the letter.

Word of Mouth:

A Quick Story

In an effort to reach as many local stores as I could in one shot, I made a list of all the stores I thought my company, The Imperial Drifter, would be a good fit for. I sent a letter, much like the one prior, along with samples.

A few months later I received an email from a men's salon in downtown Kansas City, ready to take an order. I had never heard of them. They were not in the list of businesses I sent letters and samples to. After connecting with the men's salon and providing them their initial order, I asked how they heard about The Imperial Drifter™. The store director told me, "All the guys that operate one of the stores you sent samples to get their hair cut here. They already had too many brands like The Imperial Drifter, so they couldn't purchase from you yet, so they passed it along to me."

Even if your cold calling and sample giveaways don't immediately or directly appear fruitful, you just never know. Keep trying, even if you receive an initial no. Every few months you can always try again. And, the worse thing anyone can ever tell you in sales is "No." And that's okay. **The key to sales is to never give up.**

Sales Reps

Unlike actually having to hire an employee to take care of sales, with a sales representative you are taking no *initial* risk until the representative begins producing revenue, because you're not responsible for health and retirement benefits, payroll taxes and all other cost incurrences from having employees.

Giving a sales rep a commission on each sale may seem like a lot, but depending on your situation, it might be worth it if you want to test the market, or if your product will benefit from a demonstration, or your customers require constant explanation of new products.

Things to Consider

Finding a rep to meet the exact needs of your company and to produce for you isn't as easy as it might sound. Not all sales reps produce in high numbers. This means you might have to place a lot of reps in a lot of different locations in order to squeeze the most out of your sales initiative, especially if your aim is to wholesale on a regional or national scale. But even if you just need one, they can still be hard to find.

The Agreement

Once you have found the perfect rep(s), the next step is to have them sign an Independent Sales Representative Agreement. **Independent sales reps are not employees of your business**.

The rate of commission is the number one term you want to negotiate. In our industry, a typical rate is about 15 percent of the sale. It might be hard to negotiate a rate that is lower than this industry standard, especially if you want a top quality salesperson, but I would certainly try, as 15 percent out of your wholesale revenue is considerable, depending on your situation.

Exclusivity is also an important consideration when working with independent sales reps. While you want to find reps with lots of expertise and experience in our industry, you don't want them to conflict with any of your competitors. If you're selling soap, you don't want a sales rep who represents another soap company. You must also reach an agreement about contract termination if the person fails to complete his or her responsibilities.

Finally, and in my opinion most importantly, create an agreement whereby constant communication is being conducted by the sales rep to you.

Chapter Summary

— As previously covered in Chapter 7, prepare a simple, yet nicely designed wholesale catalog listing products and prices. Make it neat and well organized, and make sure there will be enough products available to back up what is listed.

— Try to find out individual buyers' expectations of volumes and prices to see if they match your capabilities before approaching them.

— Send your catalog to buyers whose expectations best match what you have to offer. Buyers often prefer to see this before they talk to a soapmaker. You can fax it or email it to the buyer's office.

— Project a professional image. Be well informed about production, supply, product condition, etc. I have seen soapmakers with the attitude and selling approach to the tune of "Ah shucks, you don't wanna buy soap from me, do ya"? No. No we don't! Instead, be professional and exude confidence.

— Work out the details of the sale with the purchasing manager including volume, size, price, delivery dates, and labeling requirements. Many buyers have a set of written requirements for all vendors to fill out.

— Keep in touch with the buyer. Soapmakers need to keep the purchasing manager informed about anything and everything that might affect their supply chain.

You will be as successful at sales as you ultimately want to be. There will be times that you stumble along the way, say the wrong thing or just plain don't call. That's okay. We all have these moments. But momentum in selling is incredibly important and should not be overlooked.

Sometimes you have to feel the fear and do it anyway. If you don't feel like making calls or checking up on an existing wholesale customer, tough. This is your job, your business. Making sales will afford you the life you want. After all, you own a soap business. Make a list of people to call, write and offer samples to. Then get busy doing it, no excuses.

Finally, you can find and download a very thorough sales representative contract agreement at www.entrepreneur.com.

Chapter 10

Aftermarketing

Early on in my business, I made the mistake of solely focusing on churning through new leads and attaining new customers without giving the proper time and heart to my existing customers. **I lost a few along the way because of this.**

Aftermarketing has everything to do with relationship building in the world of wholesale. As previously stated, wholesaling is about the long-term. It is easy to get caught up in making sale after sale from potential leads and stockpiling your successes like an angler stockpiles his catches and focuses on the next one. But the concept of aftermarketing suggests that you not abandon your buyers after the purchase. Rather, the sale should be the start of a long-term, respectful relationship between you and the buyer.

The concept of aftermarketing has become very prominent in large business firms across the nation, as I am not the only one to have made the mistake of disregarding existing customers. The term "conquest marketing" is the antithesis of aftermarketing, suggesting that you exclusively focus on new potential leads. Because this has become such a problem in the business world, large corporations have dedicated huge teams of people within a firm to solely work with current customers (aftermarketing). **Thus, while conquest marketing is the immensely important mission to attain new retail outlets, the *retention* of current customers is unmistakably of equal importance.**

Reevaluation for the Reorder

The first evaluation took place during the initial sale. When a customer reorders your product for the first time, they have been **reevaluating** your company and your products. The reevaluation point is where current customers, for the first time, will reassess their satisfaction with your company and your products. Most importantly, they will size up their satisfaction of their experience with your business with another like-minded business, for it is human nature to do so. Their evaluation of your company will be in direct competition with your competition. **The reevaluation stage is your opportunity to shine.**

When you feel it is an appropriate time to contact the buyer for the first time since the initial sale (this will depend on how big your opening order is, the number of customers they have, etc.), find out as much information as you can. If you are local to the store, drop by and count how many bars of soap are left on the shelf, based off the initial invoice. When making contact with the buyer for the first time since the initial sale, email or telephone them first to see when a good time is to talk in person. Usually the early morning is best, as there are generally less customers they have to tend to during that time. Be prepared to work around *their* timetable, not yours. This will ultimately strengthen the relationship. You should get in front of your buyer as much as you possibly can throughout the course of doing business with him/her. If it is not feasible to drop by due to distance, telephone or email your buyer to see how things are going, and ask what you can do to enhance the current partnership.

Incentivizing Reorders

The Local Customer

On the local level, it is much easier to take care of the needs of your wholesale customer. When available (which you should make time for each week or month), you can check up on the store's stock of your products and just simply swing by to say hello to the purchasing manager. Furthermore, there are two very easy things you can do to incentivize reorders in local stores:

1) Samples

I have found that giving out samples to end-consumers in a retail outlet not only increases sales, but also makes the purchasing managers incredibly happy. Doing this assures the buyer that you are committed to the success of the initial sale and agreement you have made with them.

The best time to give away samples to end consumers is typically the store's busiest day, which in most cases is Saturday. When my company gives out samples, we tend to do so on Saturdays from 10 a.m. to 2 p.m. This will require some upfront work on your part, but I have found that it ultimately pays off with more and more reorders.

Giving Out Samples:

Agree with the purchasing manager on the most effective time giving out samples will be, in accordance with your best availability.

Find out if the purchasing manager has a table you can use, and agree upon the very best location within the store. This should be preferably as close to your store stock as possible. If they do not have a table, make sure to tell them the size of table you will bring, as they must keep in mind the access customer's are entitled to in their store.

When everything is agreed upon, prepare your samples. With soap, I always try to make at least six samples from a full bar. This is ultimately up to you. Do not give out samples of anything that the store doesn't offer. This would be undercutting your wholesale customer, and could create distrust.

Make sure to have appropriate and applicable signage and marketing materials on the table. When

206

approached by a store customer, ask them if they would like a sample, and perform your standard sales pitch. **Make sure to direct them to where your products are in the store.**

On many occasions giving out samples at stores, after packing up my table, the purchasing manager is ready to take a reorder. Because the customers that took soap samples were directed to the shelves where my products were stocked, they would often would pick up a bar or two to purchase. Thus, make sure to have enough finished product to restock at this time, so as not to have a depleted shelf of inventory when you are ready to leave for the day.

2) Simplify the Process

Depending on the size and type of retail outlet you are selling to, you can simplify the process of reordering by doing some of the grunt work for the purchasing manager, saving them time and effort.

The easiest way to do this on the local level is to drop by the store and inventory your products. It will help to bring the previous invoice so you know exactly how much was initially purchased. You can then relay this information to the purchasing manager, exposing to him/her that perhaps it is time for a reorder based on what is low in stock.

Reorder Form

Carrying with you a **reorder form** is a great way to incentivize an immediate repurchase on the local level. A reorder form is a one to two page, preprinted form with a list of your products and an area to write down the current stock as of the date inventoried, along with an area to place an order, per product. Filling out a reorder form and handing it to the purchasing manager to look over shows them that you care about the success of both parties.

Before supplying your purchasing manager a reorder with an accompanying filled-out reorder form, ask first if this method will suffice to their liking. If you are given the green light to restock and fill out the form, do so and then get their signature on the form and ask if they would make a copy for your records. This is standard procedure, and they are used to performing this task for vendors. Finally, ask them if they would still like a formal invoice, as opposed to just the reorder form. It really depends on the store. For some, the reorder form will act as an invoice, and for others you will have to duplicate what you have done into your invoicing software and then either drop it off or email it to them.

If the reorder form will suffice as an invoice for a purchasing manager, make sure you know the next invoice number in line according to your records, and enter that known number on your reorder form. For their record keeping, the store will want to memo the check they write to you with the order's invoice number.

The Non-Local Customer

There are really only three ways to incentivize reorders for the non-local customer, by email, telephone and letter. Writing letters is a bit dated when all we have to do is jump online and shoot an email. I personally have never written a letter to a company after the initial purchase has been made. I tend to stick with emailing and phone calling as my two main methods of customer service. However as a storeowner I have received written letters from local vendors and I must say it is a nice touch, and I often reordered based on the letter. Whether you write a letter or send an email, here is a pretty standard-issued correspondence I typically start with when I feel like it is appropriate to begin the reordering conversation:

Dear Alice,

Hello Alice! This is Benjamin from Prairie Soap Company. It has been a few weeks since last we spoke and I just wanted to check in on you and the store. How are things going? How is business?

I want to say first and foremost, thank you again for investing in our company and I can't wait to hear about the progress. We certainly appreciate your business and I would like to suggest that now may be a great time to reorder, as our experience shows that the time period allotted between your first order and today is just about the time when inventory starts to get low for most of our other customers.

At your convenience, let me know what you need and we will get you set up pronto.

Alice, thank you for the continued confidence in our business and I look forward to hearing from you. If you have any further questions and you need to talk, feel free to call me any time.

Keep being great,
Benjamin D. Aaron
Managing Partner, Prairie Soap Company LLC
816.352.8206

I would then typically give Alice 72 business hours to call or email me back before I telephoned her. This way, if I do end up having to call, she isn't blindsided by my contacting her. Chances are she has seen the email and just hasn't got around to emailing me back. This has always worked great for our business, and we typically receive a reorder within a week to ten days after this type of dialogue.

Of course there is always the option to simply call from the start and skip the email altogether. Keep in mind that if you do email and they don't respond in 72 hours, there still should be a phone call, so contact will be made either way. I have found that emailing first works best, even though I typically have to call. This gives them time to think about the reorder and perhaps even compile it in the interim.

Directly after the initial sale, I recommend telling your new customer that you are going to contact them in a few weeks, and then ask them if they would prefer a phone call or email.

Promotional Peps

Whether local or distant, a great way to create a lot of positive buzz around your company and products is to donate company t-shirts, hats, pens, etc. for the staff members that run a particular store where you are selling. This is a great way to say thank you for the business-to-business interaction, but it will also allow for conversation pieces within the staff and among the customers of the store. It is a goodwill gesture that will ultimately end up being a positive for your business.

Every time I have done something like this, I expensed the marketing materials (shirts, hats, pens, etc.) to advertising and promotion and always received a thank you, great feedback and lots of reorders. It is always worth doing when I feel my company can afford the advertising and promotion expense.

Every Customer is Different

Every retail outlet is different; so make sure to ask each one specifically how you should approach a reorder directly after the first sale. Some larger chain outlets will email you an official purchase order as an attachment in an email. Some smaller shops will just need you to call or come by, depending on location. Some purchasing managers want to be part of every single decision, and will let you know it. Others will love you for taking care of it all for them. Everyone is different, so make sure to ask how you can meet his or her needs and make sure to chronicle every interaction somewhere.

I personally have never used an official CRM (Customer Relationship Management) program, but I can see how helpful they could be as a client list grows and there are many to keep track of solely by memory. I do have a system in place for my company's interactions with each customer, and I know if I didn't, too many things would fall through the cracks. **Do what works best for you and your business to keep track of all the details of each customer.**

Customer Service, Defined by the Customer

I am surprised by how many handcrafted soap companies establish a customer service initiative without ever talking to their wholesale customers in an open and helpful way. To know what a customer wants, you have to ask them. **There is a lot of energy that goes into making an initial sale, but there should be just as much energy that goes into the customer and his/her needs after the first sale has been finalized**. Customer service is meeting the needs and expectations of the customer **as defined by the customer, not you.**

As previously mentioned, you enter a world of fierce competition when wholesaling handmade artisan soap. Fierce competition means that even the smallest companies are turning to quality of service as a way to distinguish themselves from the rest. Talk to your customers. Based on your conversations, determine what is most important to them and how you can further add value for them. When you become an extension of the company you sell to, it becomes inconvenient and troublesome for that company to break away from you and change vendors.

Chapter Summary

— Aftermarketing has everything to do with relationship building in the world of wholesale.

— While conquest marketing is the immensely important mission to attain new retail outlets, the *retention* of current customers is unmistakably of equal importance.

— The reevaluation point is where current customers, for the first time, will reassess their satisfaction with your company and your products.

— Be prepared to work around *their* timetable, not yours.

— Incentivizing Reorders:

Locally:

   — Samples

   — Simplify the Process

Non-Local

   — Email

   — Letter

   — Telephone

— Every customer is different.

— Customer service is meeting the needs and expectations of the customer **as defined by the customer, not you.**

Chapter 11

Build Relationships

Define Success

Nowadays, you can go Anywhere, USA and find a shelf filled with handmade soap and bodycare products. Who supplies these handmade delicacies? We do! Our industry has come on strong in recent years, and the marketplace proves it. As a cottage industry we can compare our wholesaling intentions to a local organic farmer who wishes to sell her produce to a local retailer. The local farmer doesn't have the financial backing or economic clout as big agro-industries, and we don't either. But little by little, the farmer is selling her produce into retail outlets, and so we, too, are selling our soaps.

While many purchasing managers in retail outlets across the country prefer handmade soap to synthetic detergent bars, factors including quality and price can limit their willingness to carry our products. My belief is, if soapers who collaborate together in an unusual form of competition through the use of this book and other selling concepts, we may all eventually fare better in this market, as there are more of us than them (purchasing managers). **We can set the tone with the way in which we sell our soap and bodycare products because we aren't going anywhere, and the retail outlets know this.**

Buyers' Point Of View

According to many purchasing managers I have spoken to while writing this book, their customers adore handmade soap because of its uniqueness and the opportunity it offers to support local and/or small business. Purchasing managers also appreciate the fact that handmade soapmakers can usually get products to market faster than the larger, more clunky, mass-produced soapmaking companies.

There are several key issues that purchasing managers in retail outlets will raise in regards to working with handcrafters attempting to sell on a consistent basis in their stores. **Quality is the most important issue cited by most purchasing managers**. Consistency in the quality and appeal of the soap and bodycare product means predictability. Purchasing managers love predictability, as often they are working with dozens of different vendors with dozens of different issues.

The single biggest challenge for soapmakers just starting out who decide to market to retail stores, is the consistency of their products. Purchasing managers want each box and shipment to contain items of the same size and quality. If a customer likes a product, he or she will want to return to the store and buy it again.

Product standardization goes beyond providing soap of a uniform shape and size. It also includes packaging, labeling and usually barcodes. So the handcrafted soapmaker must address how they will package their soap and bodycare products to meet individual buyers' requirements.

Price, of course, is another key issue with purchasing managers. At this point, we realize that the economy of scale and ingredients used in commercially massed-produced soaps make them cheaper than we can comprehend. So even with our handmade soaps at a higher price, many retail stores and purchasing managers *will* purchase them because of their uniqueness and the fact that customers willingly buy these items, however price should always be diligently researched and developed.

Honesty and integrity are key issues for purchasing managers in regards to building a solid relationship with handmade soap vendors. For example, if a soapmaker has a problem meeting an order commitment, the purchasing manager will want to be notified rather than having to discover it on their own. Maintaining good communication results in fewer losses of money and trust for purchasing managers. Purchasing managers want to cultivate their relationship with their vendors, especially if they are small, cottage producers such as us. I've befriended many of my purchasing managers; taking them out for drinks and having them come to visit my store. This helps them learn more about my operation and ultimately strengthens our relationship.

There are many opportunities for soapmakers to market their soaps to retail outlets. Each soapmaker should explore the marketing arrangements that

work best for them, keeping in mind that "small" handcrafters still need to provide purchasing managers with the same level (if not better) of service that larger companies do.

Define Your Own Success

By now, you have garnered many of the wholesaling concepts. Within these pages, you may or may not have gathered that wholesaling soap is incredibly objective and different for everyone, as every retail outlet is unique (not to mention the purchasing managers of each retail outlet can be drastically different). Unfortunately, there isn't a clear-cut, step 1, 2, 3, etc… that you can trust to be the way you sell. However, the previous chapters *have* covered all of the main concepts and issues that will certainly come up while wholesaling. Chapter 11 however, will allow for some mind wandering and a bit of visualizing on your part in order to better understand that the last six letters of satisfaction are ACTION.

Your Mindset And Your Business

However your business is set up, you are the Chief. You are the Commanding Officer. What you say, do and think about your business will ultimately manifest in your business.

As the Commanding Officer, I am sure you understand the inherent value of goal setting in steering your growing business in the right direction. Alas, what I have seen from many soapmakers/business owners is that they have a dreadful time determining the right direction, and the road map to get there.

The 4th Annual Staples National Small Business Survey unearthed that more than 80 percent of the 300 small business owners surveyed don't keep track of their business goals, and 77 percent have yet to achieve their vision for their company. I don't know about you, but I was in that unfortunate statistic in the early years. It wasn't until I involved myself in a serious amount of introspection into what really would make my business thrive, did I start to see the light of day. Devoting the proper amount of time to do this can sometimes seem difficult, but your business without goals is like a canoe without paddles.

Self-Efficacy In Business And Life

You are the thoughts you think. Let's repeat that. You are the thoughts you think. What you tell yourself dictates the life you lead. Whether you're an aspiring entrepreneur, or an established soap and body care business owner, your actions, opinions and words are all preceded by thought. So what are you thinking? What are you telling yourself?

The ability you have to think highly of yourself will have profound effects on your business success. **In business, the number one correlation between high sales success and any other quality is high self-esteem**. You, as the leader of your business, are involved in sales on some level. Common professional knowledge articulates that the more you like yourself, the more you like your customers. And the more your customers like you, the more they will buy from you.

Self-Esteem

When you like yourself and believe in your abilities, you:
— Set big goals.
— Persist longer in the pursuit of your big goals.
— Set high standards for your life.

— Adhere to your unique set of values and are true to whom you are.

— Refuse to compromise on your values.

If you do not currently think that highly of yourself, or if you occasionally have bouts of low self-esteem, welcome to the club. We all have trying times. We all have mishaps and we all make mistakes.

Furthermore, there is plenty outside of our business that can keep us stressed and cause anxiety, which can creep into our daily business routines and to-dos. But anything and everything can be learned and developed, including new methods of positive thought that can then be turned into daily habits. Creating new, fruitful and successful habits should not be seen as glib or simplistic – it is not easy to form new ways of doing things when your old, negative way is established and well defined.

When developing a new successful habit, keep it simple. Do not try to change yourself overnight. Doing so will cause a capitulation back into old negative thought patterns. If you worked hard on developing one new successful habit every quarter, in five years you would be doing 20 successful things every single day. Be good to yourself through this process and focus on these simple aspects to improve your psyche, which will vastly improve your revenue.

Positivity Breeds Success

Habits of Successful Business Owners

Habit #1

Successful Business Owners Read!

If you want to change your thought patterns to be more positive and uplifting, read professional journals, books and trusted web sources on business psychology, self-esteem and goal-setting. Here is a short list of books that I have read and re-read that completely changed my life. I use them as references and reminders daily:

— "Happiness for No Reason" by Marci Shimoff
— "Breaking the Chain of Low Self-Esteem" by Marilyn J. Sorensen
— "The Success Principles" by Jack Canfield
— "The 10X Rule" by Gordon Cardone

Habit #2

Successful Business Owners Are Self-Appreciative.

Appreciation is one of the highest emotional states you can possibly be in. I believe this to be the purest form of what true wealth really is. Physics and psychology both tell us that like attracts like. Being truly appreciative and showing gratitude for what you have will attract more to be grateful for. So start this process with yourself. Adore, cherish, appreciate and be grateful for you. Somehow we have been culturally conditioned to focus on what isn't so great about our lives, including our own self. But you run a business; therefore you are automatically put in a different category than the majority of working adults in the United States and developed countries. You simply cannot afford to not be grateful, appreciative and loving towards yourself.

Self-compassion breeds success. The most lucrative businesses in the soap and body care industry have leaders who are compassionate towards others. And as we all know, compassion must first be directed inward before it can ever be showcased in the direction of others.

Simply tell yourself every day how much you like, love, and are proud of you. If you have never done this before, it may feel funny at first. This is normal. But I encourage you to literally give yourself immense words of adoration and praise every day. If you do this without fail for at least 30 days, you will find that your life feels much different, and your business will have a new, fresh approach that comes from the heart.

Habit #3

They Know How To Be Present.

There is nothing worse than a leader who gives you their time but not their focus. As a successful business owner in this industry, you cannot afford to do this. You can't be everywhere for everyone, every time. There are too many variables that are beyond your control to grasp. What you can focus on is the now. The most successful of us have the ability to focus solely on one task at a time until it is either completed or the desired workload for the time is finished.

Many of us are proud of our prowess in multitasking, and wear it like a badge of honor. But more and more research suggests that the more we multi-task, the more we wear ourselves down emotionally and physically. You as the groundbreaker of your business must learn to tame the frenzy around you through organization, learning to be quiet (reflection, contemplation), and taming your surroundings. To focus on one task at a time is becoming a lost art, but not for the successful, positive business owner in our industry.

Habit #4

They Avoid the Slippery Slope of Comparison.

When people use comparison as a means of self-evaluation or business-evaluation, those who lean towards feeling inferior generally only compare themselves to people who:

— Have accomplished more.
— Are better known in the industry.
— Are more successful (or at least appear to be).
— Have more money (or at least appear to have).
— Etc…

Never feel less adequate and never berate yourself. You will only produce more negative self-statements, which will in-turn wound yourself and your business.

Time Management

What does self-esteem and success have to do with time management? **You manage your time in the absolute best way possible when you truly value yourself.** People who don't like themselves could care less about their time on Earth. Everything we do in business and life revolves around time. The quality of your life is determined by the quality of how you manage your time. Everything we have, everything we are, and everything we ever will be is a direct result of our time management. Time is the sun, and all of your goals, objectives and activities are in orbit around this meta-action.

Quite simply, business is trading. **You as the business owner don't necessarily trade products for money,** *but more your time.* You trade your time for money. So it becomes infinitely more important to create an effective environment for using your spiritual, mental, emotional and physical time and then exchange it for financial compensation.

Five Elements of Time Management

1) Build An Atmosphere Beneficial for Efficiency.

Organize, organize, organize. 30 percent of the working day is spent looking for misplaced items, folders, files, etc. That is 20 minutes out of every hour. Even if you don't feel as if you have the time, spending a considerable amount of energy consolidating and organizing your surroundings at the beginning of every week, will greatly improve your performance over time and reduce stress.

2) Set Priorities.

Make a plan for each and every day, and then win the day by knocking out your agenda. Don't overwhelm yourself with master to-do lists. Just write down three to five things you want to accomplish and work hard to do so. If you finish your list and still have time for more, do so.

3) Avoid Brain Freeze.

Complete all small tasks immediately. Divide a much larger task into smaller tasks that can immediately be worked on. Your brain will shut down if there are hundreds of things to be done. Get everything out on paper and organized as quickly as possible so they can be managed.

4) Don't Do Things That Don't Turn Into Money.

When you are working for your soap and body care company, spend your time on things that will create profit. Yes, we all need a social media presence, but there is no need for excess time spent on Facebook™, Twitter™, etc. Be as productive as possible when it is time to work on your business. This will create more enjoyment when it is time to relax and enjoy life outside of work.

5) Prime Time

Our body clocks are all different, so find out when your mind-body connections are the most creative. This is called your "prime time." Your prime time is when you are most alert and most productive. You must take advantage of this time and listen to your body. For most people, morning is prime time, but it could be different for you. Listen, feel and be reflective of when you work best and base your time around that.

Also be aware of external prime times, i.e. your customer. Make sure you know when your customers are at their prime time. In my business, we deal with regional buyers and store managers on a daily basis. Their prime time is generally between 6 a.m. and 1 p.m., as during this time they are focused on inventory and what needs to be purchased. My calling them in this window of time benefits both businesses. I would never call a wholesale customer at 4 p.m. in the afternoon, as their day is almost over and they are dealing with payroll, time sheets, etc. Use your prime time to your advantage, and try to match your customers' prime time as well.

Success Dynamics

Let's Back Up a Bit...

Below is a list of eight success dynamics that are essential to running a successful soap and body care business. But in order for these factors to offer their highest value, you must first visualize, quantify and scribe what success is for you.

Take out your magic wand and write out in detail what you want your successful life to look like. You must quantify everything in great detail. If you were ultra-successful in this industry, what does that look like? What does that *feel* like?

— How much money do you make?

— What does your bank account look like?

— What is your presence in the industry?

— What are your accolades in the industry?

— What is your family life like? Your relationships?

— Where is your career going from this successful venture?

— What are you doing to help your community?

— What is your personal enjoyment?

— What and where is the root of your happiness?

— What are the key components to healthy balance in your life?

— Are you healthy? What does that look like? What does that feel like?

— Who are your customers? What are they buying?

— What have you gotten into?

— What have you gotten out of?

— What was your big breakthrough that got you to this new level of success?

All of this should be written down. Be bold enough to do just that. It takes courage to write out in great detail what you want, but do not yet currently have. This is the first step towards greatness. Success doesn't just happen to people. **You have to want it**. And in our mushrooming industry, you have to prove that you want it by writing it out in great detail, or you will get pushed aside by someone who does have his or her objectives clearly envisioned and written down. It's your life, your success. Own up to it. It is your responsibility to create a positive, well-balanced and successful life. And if you own a company or organization, it is your ethical obligation to be as successful as possible.

Eight Success Dynamics

1) Education and Ongoing Learning

We live in a knowledge-based society. Your brain makes you money! If someone in our industry makes more money than you and is more successful, it is because they know more than you do. That's it. You can create as many scenarios, reasons and excuses as you want, but the overall state of things suggests that if you learn more, you earn more. I cannot emphasize this enough in the soap and bodycare industry. Intellectual property should be valued just as high as that organic coconut oil you have your eye on. Self-motivated learners win at life. Continue to read, research and convene with experts about the topics and advances in our industry.

2) Skill Development

The level of your ability in our field will yield the quality of your results. Going to conferences, learning new techniques, and asking the right questions to the right people will get you ahead faster than just solely relying on trial and error. As you increase your skill level, you get better at doing the small things that ultimately leads to huge productivity in your business. Generally speaking, you should have a foundational knowledge of average profit margins for popular products sold in our field. With that knowledge, you must constantly develop the skill to make things faster, more efficiently and affordable without denigrating any value, creative or otherwise. This increases your margin, one developed skill at a time.

3) Contacts

Every major change in your life is almost always accompanied by a person or persons who either open or close doors for you. The possibility of achieving the absolute best life for you will be determined by the number of people who know you, like you and are willing to help you. You can't do this alone. And even if you have started your soap and body care business through your personal creative touch, you must learn to shed the ego's grip and be willing to listen and be open to new ideas. There is a direct relationship between the right people you know and how successful you are.

My life completely changed when I met Amanda Gail of the Lovin' Soap Project. Shortly after we met for the first time, Amanda asked me to join her in going to Haiti to teach women how to make soap. I jumped at the chance and quickly learned through her leadership, both vocally and by example, what true feminism is – you must take action to call yourself a feminist. Saying the words is not enough. This shift into now co-directing a 501c3 Not-For-Profit Organization was a major change in my life, and it is due to my openness to making new contacts and opening a door that I didn't even know I had (www.lovinsoapproject.org).

This is an example of an open-door contact. You may also greatly benefit from closing doors to the people in your life that are not benefiting you in any way.

Contacts: Networking

Networking is a big buzzword in business circles these days. I could not agree more with its importance, especially in the soap and body care industry. Thanks to a globalized planet through the World Wide Web and the fact that we are indeed still a cottage industry, the ability to network and create new associates, colleagues and partners is much easier than ever before. And there is a technique to networking:

4) Always Be Of Service.

Send a new or aspiring industry comrade a customer. Rave about them.

Do something genuine and meaningful for them. Sow seeds. It all comes back to you.

Most importantly, listen more than you talk. **I would venture to recommend that in almost every social situation, listen more than you talk**. You get to take home far more feedback and learn from it than you ever would by being the one that does all the talking. This is especially true for your relationships with customers.

5) Save Your Money

You are only as free as your options. You have no freedom in life if you can't leave a situation when and how you want to. A lack of money can handcuff you and your business to a bad situation and circumstance. I am overwhelmed at how many business owners do not keep money in their business checking account. Save every penny you can in your business. If it can wait, then wait.

Develop a strong mindset of frugality towards your business funds. Keep growing it, especially in the young years of your business, as it will pay off gorgeously in the end.

"If you cannot save money, then the seeds of greatness are not in you."

6) Positive Mental Attitude

I believe this to be the most important of all eight success dynamics. You must learn through practicing healthy daily habits, to become so positive that others truly want to help you in your business. Remember, we can't do this alone. Being positive and exuding this onto others will in turn create an increasing flow of revenue.

Positive Mental Attitude: E+R=O

In his bestselling book, *The Success Principles*, Jack Canfield creates an easy approach to a very difficult concept for some people. His equation, $E+R=O$ is a constant reminder that you have the power to change how you feel about any circumstance, event or person in your life, where E is the Event, R is your Response, O is the outcome. Any event that is out of your control does not dictate your attitude, whether positive or negative. It is your response to the event that dictates your outcomes. Therefore you must take 100 percent responsibility for your thoughts, opinions, reactions and responses to all people, circumstances and events that occur in your life. You have to be the positive-minded decision maker as the leader of your soap and body care business, even if it is a business of one. The onus is on you to decide your attitude, no one else.

You become what you do. If you engage in positive actions, you will be a positive person. If you engage in negativity, gossip and generally overreact rather than respond, then you will be a negative person. Always remember that mistakes make you human. And if you own your mistakes, you instantly become more likeable and endearing. This goes a long way in the business world, especially in a business world where you sell what you craft with your own hands. Your ability to look for the good in every situation says a lot about who you are as a business owner.

As the company head, you don't get to have the miserable luxury of complaining about things. On some level you became (or aspired to become) an entrepreneur because of the freedoms, therefore, the responsibility is on you to create that scenario for yourself and your

240

employees. Complaining should never cross the corners of your mouth. Leave that to other people. You have it good. Count your blessings and remember how good you have it compared to the rest of the world.

Positive Image

Like it or not, people will judge you on appearance. But far more importantly, people will judge you by how you present yourself. Do not worry about being attractive by the common social verdicts on beauty. Be attractive through your body language and presence. This is true attraction, and it can most certainly be applied in the business world. You teach people how to treat you by how you carry yourself. In our world behind the keyboard, this dynamic gets buried, but I believe it to be ever important to present yourself in a positive, confident manner. Hold your head up, literally. Stick your shoulders out. Be proud of the only body you have to move around the world in. Body language is just that – it is a very true and real language that you communicate with.

7) Massive Creativity

Continually look for better ways to improve your business. Failing to do this is like driving with the emergency brake on. You might have all the aspirations in the world to make a successful life through your soap and body care business, but having an inadequate flow of creativity will grind your emotional and mental energies to a halt. Find out what others are doing well, conceptualize it, and then morph these concepts into your own creation and process.

All it takes is one good idea. Fortunes are made every year by companies built on a single product. What is yours? If not a product, it could be a new and interesting approach to the consumer. It could be a risky branding scheme. Whatever this idea may be, it must come from a point of originality and imagination. Find out what inspires you through some contemplation and quiet reflection. You cannot copy and paste someone else's business ideals and motivations and expect it to work for you. The Business Gods do not reward this. Come original. Do you. Originality breeds success. Business guru Barbara Corcoran simply goes outside for a walk when she feels that she or her business has reached a point of stagnation. Sometimes this is all it takes. Carve out some time and energy in your week to allow creativity to flow. It's good for the soul.

242

8) Character

People may doubt what you say, but they will always believe what you do. Most of us have an uncanny ability to detect rubbish. Even people with great personalities can be full of it. So it is your job as a successful business owner to not only have great personality, but have a deep and gripping character. Personality is often easy to read, and it is the first thing presented to our senses when meeting someone. Personality has everything to do with how funny or serious, amicable or rude, introverted or extroverted, etc. someone is.

Keep in mind that in the world of social media, we often will catch glimpses of personalities. But what is not always perceived as quickly is the character of a person. I see the personality of an individual as the part of a tree you can see above the ground and the character is the root system. Both are equally important to a blossomed success. Having a deep and gripping character means you have the traits of honesty, virtue and kindness. It is your job to introduce your customer to the personality of your business (your products), but make sure they have the ability to obtain the character of your business as well. This is done through your mission statement and values, but more importantly, how you treat them and take care of them in the long-term. Repeat customers are independently seeking out your business because they have a developed sense of your character.

In Sales and Business,

Always Remember…

Being likeable does not mean that everyone will like you. Yes, your products are wonderful and your personality is great and character deep, but you will get no's. And the more you put yourself out there, the more likely it is to get no's, simply because that is what statistics tell us. But at the end of the day you must understand that this is a numbers game, and the amount of no's and yes's that you receive are not who you are when your head hits the pillow. Everyone in our industry experiences rejection.

Your peers, employees, partners and especially customers will only respect you to the degree that you demonstrate a strong respect for yourself.

The End.

About The Author

Benjamin Aaron is an avid soapmaker. With his mother, Sheila, being a soapmaker, he grew up with handmade soap and was taught how to craft it at an early age. With a handful of goals and absolutely zero business experience, he has carved out a very nice living through selling soap and bodycare products.

Prairie Soap Company, LLC

Benjamin has been handcrafting soap and body care products since 2009 and quickly turned this learned hobby into a burgeoning business. Prairie Soap Company, LLC was the first real high-revenue achievement in Benjamin's career. With the help of his family, he started

Prairie Soap Company in his parent's kitchen after his luck had run out working a trade that was grueling, inflexible and well, not *his*. After making two batches of soap with the help of his beautiful mother Sheila, he wanted to start a business. Badly. And of course, everyone thought he was nuts (Sound familiar?). At 24 years old, Benjamin decided that he no longer needed a resume or a nice suit for a job interview. He was going to make a living by making and selling soap.

And he has never looked back. Benjamin has been working for himself since the age of 24 and his career in the entrepreneurial field of soapmaking has brought him the kind of triumph and success that shines on the heart and soul. Like many soapmakers, he originally had trouble wrapping his head around revenue. He often gave away what he made and was naive about his own success in the field of handcrafted soap. But over time he came to realize that his life and career wasn't getting better because *he* wasn't getting better.

Thus, Benjamin's journey of success as a soapmaker started within himself. He began accomplishing goal after goal, ascending that once seemingly impossible climb, because he opened up a path of self-respect and learned how to be at peace with myself. **When we are at peace with ourselves, we are open to learning, failing, trying and (finally) succeeding in whatever we set out to do.**

Once this concept fermented long enough in his mind, Benjamin began making phone call after phone call, asking for the sale. He did whatever he could to increase his sales on the World Wide Web. He asked purchasing managers at retail stores how to sell. Whatever he could do to advance his business, he did it, no matter how scared he was or how many times he failed.

For years, Prairie Soap Company has resided in a retail shopping center, open 362 days out of the year, offering classes year-round to the local community. In addition to retail and education, Prairie Soap Company wholesales to large, nationwide chain retailers, such as Whole Foods Market™, Natural Grocers™, Lucky's™, Sprouts™ and The Fresh Market™.

The Imperial Drifter

Benjamin's newest for-profit company, The Imperial Drifter, utilizes the unique and abundant qualities of natural oils for the grooming needs of men, specializing in beard oil and beard balm. The Imperial Drifter has quickly become a fun and trendy business, booming with even more potential and creativity. Beards are in like they haven't been before...okay maybe at least since the 1970s. So Benjamin wanted to capitalize on this trend and did so quickly. With relatively high markups, The Imperial Drifter is well on its way to achieving great things, not the least of which is high profits.

The Lovin' Soap Project

The Lovin' Soap Project organizes soap making workshops for women in developing countries, which reduces gender violence and inequality, helps families send their sons and daughters to school and saves lives through access to hygiene. Benjamin is a proud co-director of this endearing voyage. The Lovin' Soap Project is a 501(c)(3) non-profit organization that has been actively engaged in the lives of women in developing nations for 3 years.

Countries Traveled:
— Haiti (2 groups)
— Uganda
— China (Tibet Region)

— India

Just like any for-profit organization (including Benjamin's own), the day-to-day logistical approach to progress as a women's empowerment organization has no limits. The Lovin' Soap Project has made great advances in the lives of women we have met through the education and training of soapmaking and business startup.

To all readers, I implore you to check out what the Lovin' Soap Project is up to at www.lovinsoapproject.org.

Our Handcrafted Soap Community

Benjamin recurrently gives speaking engagements at various industry events and conferences, such as:
— **The Central Soapers Workshop**
— **The Tennessee Soap & Candle Social**
— **The Handcrafted Soap & Cosmetic Guild Annual Conference**
— **The Alabama Soap & Candle Association**
— **Lovin' Soap Studio Workshops & Bootcamps**

All of Benjamin's speaking engagements have been based around the power of goal setting, truly defining success, and how the way you feel about yourself dictates your outcomes as an entrepreneur.

If you are in the know about a meeting or conference and would like Benjamin to speak, please contact me at info@howtosellsoap.com.

Thank you for reading my book.

Keep doing great things.

Benjamin D. Aaron
www.howtosellsoap.com

Glossary of Terms

Brand Management

Brand management is the analysis and planning on how that brand is perceived in the market. Developing a good relationship with the target market is essential for brand management. Tangible elements of brand management include the product itself; look, price, the packaging, etc. The intangible elements are the experience that the consumer has had with the brand, and also the relationship that they have with that brand.

Catalog (Product)

Printed or virtual materials published by manufacturing businesses. They promote sales by making advertising claims, give instructions in using products, provide testimonials from satisfied customers, and include detailed descriptions of sale products.

Cause Marketing

Cause marketing or cause-related marketing refers to a type of marketing involving the cooperative efforts of a for-profit business and a non-profit organization for mutual benefit.

Cold Calling

Cold calling is the solicitation of business from potential customers who have had no prior contact with the salesperson conducting the call. Cold calling is used to attempt to convince potential customers to purchase either the salesperson's product or service. Cold calling is generally referred to as an over-the-phone process, but can also be done in-person.

Competition (In Business)

In capitalist economics, competition is the rivalry among sellers trying to achieve such goals as increasing profits, market share, and sales volume by varying the elements of the marketing mix: price, product, distribution, and promotion.

Competitive Advantage

Competitive advantage is a business concept describing attributes that allow an organization to outperform its competitors.

Consignment

Consignment is the act of giving over to another person or agent's charge, custody or care any material or goods, but retaining legal ownership until the material or goods are sold.

Cottage Industry

A cottage industry is one where the creation of products and services is home-based, rather than factory-based. While products and services created by cottage industry are often unique and distinctive, given the fact that they are usually not mass-produced, producers in this sector often face numerous disadvantages when trying to compete with much larger factory-based companies.

Customer Service

Customer service is the provision of service to customers before, during and after a purchase.

Economy Of Scale

Economies of scale are the cost advantages that companies obtain due to size, output, or scale of operation, with cost per unit of output generally decreasing with increasing scale as fixed costs are spread out over more units of output.

Fixed Costs

In economics, fixed costs, indirect costs or overheads are business expenses that are not dependent on the level of goods or services produced by the business. They tend to be time-related, such as salaries or rents being paid per month, and are often referred to as overhead costs. This is in contrast to variable costs, which are volume-related (and are paid per quantity produced).

Goal

A goal is a desired result that a person or a system envisions, plans and commits to achieve: a personal or organizational desired end-point in some sort of assumed development. Many people endeavor to reach goals within a finite time by setting deadlines.

Manufacturing Cost

Manufacturing cost is the sum of costs of all resources consumed in the process of making a product.

Marketplace

An economy in which decisions regarding investment, production, and distribution are based on supply and demand, and prices of goods and services are determined in a free price system.

Market Research

Any organized effort to gather information about target markets or customers.

Market Value

An estimate of the market value of a property, based on what a knowledgeable, willing, and unpressured buyer would probably pay to a knowledgeable, willing, and unpressured seller in the market.

Markup (Price)

Markup is the difference between the cost of a good or service and its selling price.[1] A markup is added onto the total cost incurred by the producer of a good or service in order to create a profit. The total cost reflects the total amount of both fixed and variable expenses to produce and distribute a product.[2] Markup can be expressed as a fixed amount or as a percentage of the total cost or selling price.[1] Retail markup is commonly calculated as the difference between wholesale price and retail price, as a percentage of wholesale.

Mission Statement

A mission statement is a statement of the purpose of a company, organization or person; its reason for existing; a written declaration of an organization's core purpose and focus that normally remains unchanged over time.

Networking

A supportive system of sharing information and services among individuals and groups having a common interest.

Niche Market

The subset of the market on which a specific product is focused. The market niche defines the product features aimed at satisfying specific market needs, as well as the price range, production quality and the demographics that is intended to impact.

People Skills

The ability to communicate effectively with people in a friendly way, especially in business.

Product Line

The offering of several related products for sale individually. A line can comprise related products of various sizes, types, colors, qualities, or prices.

Profit Margin

Profit margin is a measure of profitability. It is calculated by finding the net profit as a percentage of the revenue.

Purchasing Manager

A Purchasing Manager is an employee within a company, business or other organization who is responsible at some level for buying or approving the acquisition of goods and services needed by the company. The store owner and the purchasing manager are sometimes the same person.

Purchase Order

A purchase order (PO) is a commercial document indicating types, quantities, and agreed prices for products or services.

Revenue

Income that a company receives from its normal business activities, usually from the sale of goods and services to customers.

Sales Letter

A sales letter is a piece of direct mail or an email, which is designed to persuade the reader to purchase a particular product or service in the absence of a salesman.

Sales Pitch

A sales pitch is a planned presentation of a product or service designed to initiate and close a sale of the same product or service. A sales pitch is essentially designed to be either an introduction of a product or service to an audience who knows nothing about it, or a descriptive expansion of a product or service that an audience has already expressed interest in. Sales professionals prepare and give a sales pitch, which can be either formal or informal and might be delivered in a number of ways.

Self-Efficacy

Self-efficacy is the extent or strength of one's belief in one's own ability to complete tasks and reach goals.

Success

The favorable or prosperous termination of attempts or endeavors; the accomplishment of one's goals.

Suggested Retail Price (SRP)

The suggested retail price of a product is the price at which the manufacturer recommends that the retailer sell the product. While some stores always sell at, or below, the suggested retail price, others do so only when items are on sale or closeout/clearance.

Target Market

A group of customers towards which a business has decided to aim its marketing efforts and ultimately its merchandise.

Time Management

Time management is the act or process of planning and exercising conscious control over the amount of time spent on specific activities, especially to increase effectiveness, efficiency or productivity.

Unit Cost

The cost incurred by a company to produce, store and sell one unit of a particular product. Unit costs include all fixed costs and all variable costs involved in production.

Value Perception (In Business)

The difference between a prospective customer's evaluation of the benefits and costs of one product when compared with others. Value perception may also be expressed as a straightforward relationship between perceived benefits and perceived costs:

Value = Benefits / Cost.

Variable Costs

Variable costs are costs that change in proportion to the good or service that a business produces.

Wholesale

Wholesaling is the sale of merchandise to retailers. In general, it is the sale of goods to anyone other than a standard consumer.

Resources

Soapmaking Supplies

Bramble Berry

www.brambleberry.com

Bramble Berry offers an extensive selection of soap & toiletry making products for everyone from the weekend hobbyist up to high-volume professional soap makers. You'll find base oils, colorants, exfoliants, fragrance oils, essential oils, molds, packaging, kits and more!

Elements Bath and Body

www.elementsbathandbody.com

Elements offers wholesale soap making supplies, packaging, recipes, instructions and accessories.

Essential Depot

www.essential-depot.com

Essential Depot's goal is to provide the best quality soap making ingredients, at the best possible price.

Essential Wholesale

www.essentialwholesale.com

Essential Wholesale offers cosmetic bases, essential oils, carrier oils, exotic butters & waxes, cosmetic & soap making ingredients, fruit & herbal extracts, organics and so much more.

From Nature with Love

www.fromnaturewithlove.com

From Nature With Love is a wholesale supplier of 1,750+ natural and complementary ingredients used in skin care, hair care, aromatherapy, massage, spa products, herbal preparations, soap making, potpourri and candle making.

Liberty Natural Products

www.libertynatural.com

Liberty Natural Products is a grower, importer and wholesale distributor of over 1,200 botanical ingredients and natural products.

Mad Oils

www.madoils.com

Mad Oil's goal to provide you with the highest quality products you can buy, and then back it up with unsurpassed customer service.

New Directions Aromatics

www.newdirectionsaromatics.com

NDA offers aromatherapy essential oils, cosmetic bases, candle making supplies, soap making supplies, spa products, fragrant oils, specialty packaging & more.

Peak Candle Supplies

www.peakcandle.com

Peak Candle Making Supplies offers candle making supplies, soap making supplies, fragrance oils, and starter kits, all at wholesale prices.

SFIC Corporation

www.sficcorp.com

SFIC offers high quality melt and pour soap bases.

Shay and Company

www.shayandcompany.com

Shay and Company, Inc. is a distributor of a wide selection of oils, butters and soap making products, including many types of vegetable oils, a full line of liquid soaps. several types of melt & pour soap bases and a selection of exotic butters that can be used in all types of soaps, toiletries and skin care products.

Soaper's Choice

www.soaperschoice.com

Soaper's Choice offers soapmaking base oils, butters, waxes and other ingredients. They have excellent prices on bulk orders.

Sweet Cakes Soapmaking Supplies

www.sweetcakes.com

Sweet Cakes offer soapmaking supplies, base oils, fragrance oils, flavor oils, essential oils and more.

The Herbarie

www.theherbarie.com

The Herbarie offers ingredients for the cosmetics and toiletries, personal care, spa and wellness industries.

The Lye Guy

www.thelyeguy.com

The Lye Guy offers sodium hydroxide and potassium hydroxide.

TKB Trading LLC

www.tkbtrading.com

TKB offers a wide selection of micas for coloring soap and other body products.

Wholesale Supplies Plus

www.wholesalesuppliesplus.com

WSP offers melt and pour glycerin soap base, fixed oils, butters, colors, molds, packaging, fragrance and Essential Oils.

Production / Cost Software

SoapMaker Professional

www.soapmaker.ca

CraftyBase

www.craftybase.com

Soapmaking Equipment

Soap Equipment (Willow Way)

www.soapequipment.com

Labeling Sources

Lightning Labels

www.lightninglabels.com

Leaping Lizard Labels

www.leapinglizardlabels.com

Online Labels

www.onlinelabels.com

Short Run Labels

www.shortrunlabels.com

Your Box Solution

www.yourboxsolution.com

Online Tutorials and Instructions

Lovin' Soap

www.lovinsoap.com

Amanda Gail's tutorial based soap making site. You'll find tutorials, interviews, reviews and more!

Candle and Soap at About.com

www.candleandsoap.about.com

David Fisher is your guide to the world of Candle and Soap making! He has information and tutorials on just about every process of making soap including cold process, hot process, liquid and cream!

Soap Queen

www.soapqueen.com

Anne-Marie Faiola, owner of Bramble Berry, has a wonderful blog featuring tutorials for making soap, lotion, scrubs, candles, lip balm and more! Her video series for cold process soap is probably one of the best on the Internet. You can find it at soapqueen.tv.

Wholesale Supplies Plus

www.wholesalesuppliesplus.com

Online Publications

Soap Collaborative

www.soapcollaborative.org

Saponifier Magazine

www.saponifier.com

Founded in 1998, Saponifier is an online digital magazine for soap, toiletry and candle makers.

Soapmaking Trade Organizations

Indie Business Network

www.indiebusinessnetwork.com

The Indie Beauty Network (IBN) helps independent (indie) business owners to maximize their potential through small business ownership. We are a business organization, dedicated to serving our members' business needs so they can focus on earning a fair profit and growing their companies.

Handcrafted Soap and Cosmetic Guild

www.soapguild.org

The Handcrafted Soap and Cosmetic Guild is a non-profit trade association, which works to promote and protect the handcrafted soap industry.

Soapmaking Classes

The Lovin' Soap Studio

www.lovinsoap.com